C A T S

24 hours

a day

CATS

BY WINIFRED CARRIÈRE

Photographs by
GEORGE VIERLING

GALAHAD BOOKS • NEW YORK CITY

Library of Congress Catalog Card Number: 73-92832
ISBN: 0-88365-213-7
Published by arrangement with Funk & Wagnalls, New York
Manufactured in the United States of America

TO DR. LEON J. ROTH—*my cats' best friend*

CONTENTS

C A T S

24 hours

a day

INTRODUCTION

In the early 1900's, a shy child was told, "The cat's got your tongue." I was a very shy child, and the cat got all of me. That is why I learned very early in life that any human who earns the right to say "my cat" is actually possessed by the cat. He may have bought and paid for his pet, but it is the cat who owns him—from the time the cat first decides to give the combination a try.

In rereading the manuscript, I find I have used the term "my cats" frequently. It must be regarded simply as a shorthand symbol—an easy way of referring to the little feline individualists who allow me to provide them with a home according to their directions, to feed them their preferred viands, to try to understand their complex personalities and problems, and to love them extravagantly.

As a little girl, I longed for a kitten, but according to Auntie, with whom I lived, cats belonged in the barn in which the horses' feed attracted mice. In the house, cats were untrustworthy, and furthermore might make messes.

Eventually, however, I persuaded Auntie that a kitten was not a cat and therefore could be allowed in the house on occasion; that I was old enough to make certain that the kitten made no messes; and that *I wanted one more than anything else in the world*. Auntie gave in, and at last I became slightly and briefly acquainted with Brownie. She was less than a year old when an Airedale killed her, and it was years before I had another kitten.

Now, for almost twenty years, I have happily been without a catless moment. The three who possess me currently are five-year-old Chieng Jo-Jo, four-year-old SuziTu (both Siamese), and eighteen-year-old Minnie, a "domestic shorthair" in solid black, now touched with a few snowflakes due to extreme old age. They possess me as completely as if they had bought and paid for me, as indeed each in his or her own way has done many times over. I have much to thank them for—these three and their predecessors and kinfolk.

It is because we have all got along so well together—and I think I can honestly say that my possessors have been as happy as I—that I have written this book. Many mistakes in human-to-cat relationships are based simply on misunderstanding or lack of understanding of cats and what they expect of their humans. I have made at least my full share of these mistakes and learned from every one of them. My association with cats has been entirely nonprofessional. Loving them, I have tried to learn all I could about them: from books, from small-animal doctors, from other cat lovers, and most of all, from the cats themselves.

So this book is a recounting of what I have learned and how I learned it. Because I believe so firmly in letting trained professionals handle all matters of health, I have had my manuscript thoroughly checked for accuracy in this regard by one of New York City's prominent small-animal doctors, Dr. Leon J. Roth. His expert care and understanding in times of need have contributed much to the happiness that my cats and I continue to share.

If in these pages I have given you "my-cat-does-that-too" entertainment, I have served part of my purpose. If I have given "Ah—so-*that*'s-why" cause for thought, I have served it further. In case I have given both, plus "I must remember that, because I didn't know it," I have indexed the book to make recollection easier. But I shall have fulfilled a labor of love for all felinity if I have opened even a tiny crack into the vast, beautiful, exciting experience of understanding cats.

WINIFRED CARRIÈRE

1

Cat on the Couch

The most amazing thing about cats is that very few of them actually need the psychiatrist's couch. How can they possibly endure with such equanimity the insults and abuse, intentional and unintentional, that humans inflict on them? How frustrating it must be to be so frequently misunderstood and underestimated. Perhaps they just rise above it, thinking higher thoughts and forgiving people because, after all, we are only people. And any cat can tell you that people are benighted with a most abysmal ignorance!

People who do not recognize that cats are thinking, understanding, responsive creatures of great intelligence say in bewilderment, "Why, you'd almost think he understood what was going on!" Of course the cat knows. The cat is what his people make him appear to be—happy, well-adjusted, healthy in mind and body, or neurotic and miserable.

The sympathy and empathy of which a cat is capable when he possesses a human is one of the delights of being possessed. But as I have learned from my cats, "you gets what you gives." Actually, the cat is the mirror of his human's mind, personality, and attitude, just as the dog mirrors his human's physical appearance.

The day I went to purchase Jo-Jo, for example, I met his humans for the first time. A most gracious lady opened the door, and genuine friendliness radiated from her. Behind her were two delightful little boys, equally friendly although more than a little sad at the thought of parting with their one remaining kitten. Next came Jo-Jo's parents, Chieng Ho-Ho and Chieng Leing, strolling into the room in tandem, tails waving in cordial welcome. An elderly dog nodded pleasantly to me, then went under a table in the next room to nap.

The rest of the procession approached me without fear or suspicion, expressed interest and pleasure in meeting me, and completed the picture I had quickly acquired of a happy, friendly family whose cats felt secure, understood, and loved. I knew that little Jo-Jo, still napping on the sunporch, would also respond to the welcome and love that awaited him at my home, and so he has.

Time and again I have found my cats responding plainly to my mood of the moment. When I am carefree and happy, they romp around the house as though they had just sniffed catnip. When the tune of my typewriter is a rapid, confident chatter, they come to sit beside me, grinning. "Writing about us?" they ask, looking pleased. When I let things get me down, or a chapter sits stubbornly locked in my mind, their tails are inclined to droop, their eyes look sad and questioning, and they try to comfort me with quiet little extra paw-pats and ankle-rubs of love and confidence. Others' cats, too, reflect their people's thoughts and attitudes. Susan, my teen-age friend, once threw her knee out of whack and limped about on crutches for a week or so. Although nothing whatever was wrong with Susan's tabby, Alice, she limped, too, until Susan could walk normally again.

A cat can cope with being beaten up by another cat, even though he may come limping home after several days' absence looking like a Bowery bum. It is only his body that is injured, and with your help and his own instinctively correct ministrations, he will heal. Only a human can injure a cat's spirit, and it is equally true that only a *loving*, *understanding* human can heal it.

There was the case of the two cats who lived together, one happy and well-adjusted, and the other, a psychological misfit. Their people tried in every way possible to lure the emotionally disturbed cat into a sense of security. They paid so much attention to him, in fact, that finally the other cat, seeking her share of human interest, went off into a spell of doldrums, sulking in corners and refusing to eat.

Rarely, a cat has a really deep-seated psychiatric problem. I am convinced that it is a condition that is basically people-caused, even when it can be logically traced to heredity. Monster was one of these troubled cats. I cannot even conjecture as to the origin of his difficulty, since I neither saw his original home environment nor met his mother or littermate. I did hear, after Monnie had been living with us for a couple of years and his problem had become evident, that his brother had been executed because he was vicious. I loved Monster so dearly that I could never, under any circumstances, have resorted to such an extreme action, although frightened acquaintances advised me to do so.

He got me into trouble on several occasions, and perhaps

I loved him more than I would have loved a better-adjusted cat merely because I was determined to help him. "If I can love him enough," I reasoned, "and convince him that I love him, I can cure him—or at least teach him enough self-control to stay out of trouble."

Monster was the first cat to possess me after a long spell of catlessness. He was adorable as a kitten—guttersnipe-fresh and playful, always a little boisterous. It was during his kittenhood that he showed his unbalanced attitude for the first time, and I was too inexperienced to recognize it as something serious. Possibly I could have prevented future difficulties if I had correctly diagnosed the symptoms at once.

The girl who had found him for me and brought him to me came frequently to visit. She was very cat-knowledgeable, in terms of care and feeding, and I trusted her not to do anything to Monnie that should not be done. Yet, because he was so playful and tirelessly entertaining, perhaps, she played with him for longer periods of time than a baby cat can stand. He kept up with her, instead of taking himself off for a nap when he was tired, until rather suddenly a change came over him. His eyes became enormous black pools; all the gold of the irises disappeared from around the pupils. He lunged with his sharp baby teeth and took a good, hard bite of her arm.

We thought he was cute and spunky. The next time it happened, the circumstances were similar. A young man was visiting us, and very quietly but persistently played with Monnie until once again Monnie suddenly became a little demon and sank his teeth into the young man's hand. The young man was not entirely pleased, but made no fuss about it.

As Monnie grew to maturity, he continued to be playful and to enjoy visits by my friends-of-the-inner-circle. They were his friends, too. He never thought of objecting to them, and even when there was a period of several years between visits from them, he never forgot them. It was only strangers who seemed to him to be unnecessary intruders. But in time, I learned to recognize the dilation of his black pupils as an emotional danger signal, to stop the play, and to escort the maddened little cat into exile. I did not punish him for these aberrations. I knew that he could not help himself, and at least in his young days, it was overplayful people who brought it on themselves.

Monnie recognized the difference between a social visitor and a business caller, and he welcomed the latter like old friends. So the only subterfuge I could ever get away with was the vacuum-cleaner-salesman story. Until I finally relented and invested in a new one, I at one time owned a vacuum cleaner that was constantly in need of repair. Monnie came to know the vacuum-cleaner repair man, recognized him as no social menace, and treated him with the utmost cordiality.

When someone Monster did not know came to spend an evening with me, I assured the cat that "this is a vacuum-cleaner salesman." He may eventually have discovered the hoax, but his immediate reaction was to pack away all hostilities, which gave me an opportunity to ease him out of the room. Perhaps it was unfair, because his distaste for some of those visitors was just plain good judgment.

Eventually, we worked out the solution. Whenever the doorbell rang and I was expecting anyone whom Monster did not know, I escorted him gently and quietly into another room and shut the door. He seemed grateful to be taken out of circulation. He not only went willingly to his solitude, but also developed a habit of jumping onto the shelf in my bedroom closet, which I left open for him, and sitting there calmly until the guests had departed.

When this shelving habit had become so routine that I always knew where to find him when the coast was clear, he went a step further. When the doorbell rang, Monster beat a hasty but dignified retreat and shelved himself.

Yet during the thirteen years that Monnie lived with us, there were several occasions when I could not prevent him from launching a sudden, completely vicious attack on an innocent human visitor. Always it was an arm for which he lunged; in addition to the shock value of suddenly being bitten by what had appeared to be a friendly, happy cat, the wounds he inflicted were serious. The first victim reported the matter to the police department, through the doctor who treated the wound, and I was required to take Monster to the ASPCA for examination and a clean bill of health regarding rabies. He was perfectly healthy, of course, but there are laws about cat bites.

There were a couple of other disastrous attacks, and a cat who has to be checked out for rabies at police-department instigation more than twice is confiscated and destroyed as a vicious animal. So I was careful to keep him out of the clutches of the law. The last time was really the worst, because I complicated it myself, quite unwittingly.

I had a wisdom tooth extracted, and it was complicated. The dental surgeon doped me with all sorts of antibiotics, and I turned out to be violently allergic to parabenzamine, which was included in this postoperative treatment. Because I was high as a kite on the drugs, my friend and office assistant, Kitty, decided to spend the night with me. Anne, my daughter, was away at school, so Kitty went to sleep in Anne's room.

When I heard Kitty scream, I staggered out of bed, peeled

Monster off her punctured arm, and rushed to the linen closet where I kept the medicines that were not in daily use. I poured a liberal swig of what I thought was antiseptic over Kitty's wound and went back to bed. Whatever it was that I doused her with, it was certainly not antiseptic. Kitty had her blood-poisoned arm in a sling for a week. After that, I always made certain that Monster could not get away from captivity when I had overnight guests.

Eventually, I learned the pattern and reason for Monnie's antisocial behavior. He adored me, my teen-age daughter, and my small circle of very close friends whom he saw every day. But in his devotion to us he was intensely, and at times insanely, jealous. He never attacked a loved friend or member of the family, except once when he punished Anne for something real or fancied he disapproved of. He could not—simply could not—allow us to give any prolonged attention or hospitality to someone he either did not know well or whom he disliked. Sooner or later, he sprang, out of control and with intent to do damage.

I had two approaches to the problem: One was getting him out of the way; the other was to love him and express it—to discuss the problem with him, to admonish him quietly and firmly but with sympathy and understanding, to tell him that although he could not help it, he absolutely *must* try to change. There is no vestige of doubt in my mind that he *did* try to overcome the problem. Monster was probably the most intelligent cat I have ever known, which may have influenced his occasional lapses into insanity. Like any mad genius, he may have had too good a mentality to live with as a cat. (I used to ask him whether he had previously been Napoleon or Teddy Roosevelt, but he never enlightened me.)

He was quickly over each attack, and always thoroughly,

abjectly ashamed of himself. Because of my belief that we might have avoided the problems entirely if I had exerted more sensible control over the people who teased him when he was a baby, I have always been very careful never to let anyone play too long or too hard with subsequent kittens who have lived with me. But there was obviously something fundamentally wrong—possibly hereditary, since his brother must have shown the same tendencies. I wish I knew whether or not I could have made his littermate into a socially acceptable cat, had I had the opportunity. I did it to Monster successfully, through the sheer force of loving and understanding.

Although Anne was nine when Monnie came to us, by the time she was ten, he was almost grown up. A year-old cat may still not be quite fully grown, yet ready for adult responsibilities. Consequently, Monnie took over the job of helping me bring up my daughter. He watched over her. He supervised her friendships. He swore at the young friends he did not like, adopted those of whom he approved. They all gained a healthy respect for him. Monnie was boss, even if Anne's mother was busy elsewhere.

Later, when Anne's baby was put to bed in Monnie's territory, Monnie again took over as baby-sitter. The baby loved him, too, and Monster was careful never to frighten Kurt or to say anything cross to him. Once I embarrassed Monnie no end by watching him tiptoe up to Kurt's crib, just to check that all was well and the baby was asleep as he should be. Monnie's baby-sitting was a very private matter, and he resented my spying on him.

In the years we lived together, Monster came to feel that he and I shared equally the job of bossing. On a few occasions, he took exception to my decision, and we had some touch-and-go flare-ups. They never lasted long, and they happened infrequently, because we had long ago established an understanding that went far deeper than words.

Because of our mutual understanding and respect, Monnie took responsibilities very seriously. Part of his job was to see to it that nothing I treasured should ever be disturbed or harmed. Although it was all right for *him* to scratch on the furniture, he often batted Minnie, his ever-adoring helpmate, for doing the same. So when he broke the Wedgwood, his shame knew no bounds.

It was all my fault, and I apologized profusely, explaining that he had had nothing at all to do with it, that it was an accident, and that he should not feel bad about it. He refused to be consoled. He sat himself down in a corner, face to the wall, and stayed there for a couple of hours. It really was my fault, too. We had had the apartment torn up in readiness for the painters, and I had put the Wedgwood collection on the shelf in the bedroom closet, without thinking that that particular section of that particular shelf was Monnie's hideout. Since he could not see the tissue-wrapped packages from the floor, he jumped up as usual and fell back amidst a crashing of shattered pottery. It was the first and last time that Monnie ever broke anything of mine.

I have never met another cat with recognizable symptoms of insanity, but perfectly sane cats, I have discovered, can balloon their grudges into first-class hatreds. A three-room apartment in the city simply is not large enough to accommodate a feud, but I lived with one for almost two years. What Minnie and Jo-Jo were feuding about, I do not know with certainty. My guess is that it started as a question of who was here first, you upstart; and who fathered kittens, you old hag; and who is Madam's favorite; and who runs this house, anyhow? You know—the momentous minutiae on which lifetimes and even generations of feuding are usually based.

At any rate, it began when SuziTu had her second litter of kittens. Suzi was busy and preoccupied, so Jo-Jo approached Minnie for friendly attention. He may have suggested more than friendship, for she slapped his face and snarled. Jo-Jo has an overgrown mother complex about Minnie, because he was very young when he came to live with her, and she was very old. His feelings were deeply hurt by her rebuff, and it showed in his sad blue eyes. There was a painful armed truce between them for three months, Jo-Jo trying again and again to regain Minnie's approval, Minnie continuing to build up her nothing-doing nastiness. At last one night, all hell broke loose. Suzi and Jo-Jo together got Minnie down and gave her a sound beating, and it was obvious that I could not allow them to be in the same room with her until they had all calmed down. Only they had no intention of being friends again—ever, ever, *ever!*

The immediate solution was to shut Minnie into the bedroom and keep the other two out. (The kittens, who had witnessed the battle from strategically safe hideouts, gave her wide berth.) This physical separation was no easy accomplishment, as Jo-Jo developed great agility in squeezing through the door before I could close it when I went in or out. Also, it was distressing to me on another count. We had always slept together, each cat having a favored position on my bed. I felt guilty and even a little lonely at bedtime with only Minnie, sweet as she is, sharing my slumbers. And there was a hurt look of accusation in Jo-Jo's eyes when I shut the bedroom door and left him on the outside. Nevertheless, there was nothing else I could do—or so I thought.

Months later, while I was reviewing with satisfaction the long-past memory of Monster's psychiatric problems and how I had overcome them, it dawned on me that I was *not* practicing what I preach. "If you love enough, and understand thoroughly, you can overcome this problem," I said to myself.

So I opened the bedroom door, sat down in the chair beside Minnie, and invited the eager, adoring Jo-Jo and cautious, reserved SuziTu to join us. Jo-Jo galloped headlong into the bedroom, racing toward Minnie, shouting "Hiya, Minnie-old-girl! Long time no see! Waa-how!" Naturally, he scared the daylights out of her. He really meant to be friendly, but he was so excited that he could not contain himself. She answered with frightened, snarling imprecations that set his fur on end, and they were ready to do battle again. Suzi crept out of the room, dragging her tail behind her. I talked quietly to the combatants, stroking their fur for a few moments and trying to calm them. The first session lasted about three minutes, until I picked up Jo-Jo, carted him out, and closed the door.

Each day thereafter, I held another get together, increasing the length of the visit gradually. Every time I opened the door, Jo-Jo charged in with his back-slapping greeting, and Minnie snarled from under the chair. Gradually, because I talked softly and constantly to them during these sessions, petted them all, and repeatedly complimented them individually and collectively, it became possible for me to leave the chair safely and busy myself elsewhere in the room. I kept the togetherness sessions short for a couple of weeks and finally was able to leave the room entirely—staying within a quick-return area in case of emergency. Frequently, I had to rescue Jo-Jo, who seemed determined to walk into the teeth of danger (literally) and was ashamed to retreat when Minnie warned him of her intent to annihilate him. After a time, however, I contented myself with simply going into the room when I heard the low mutter of Minnie's preliminary thunder and saying calmly, "Now cut it out, you two. You're being ridiculous." Once, I took my sketch pad with me and sketched them with their fur on edge. Oddly, this technique worked better than removing Jo-Jo bodily.

Emboldened by success with my open-door policy, policed as it was, I initiated the next step–open door at night, when they could commit mayhem to the blare of trumpets without disturbing me, once I had gone to sleep. The first night, there was a scrabble session on the bed before I had even had a chance to gather sand for my eyes, and Jo-Jo and Suzi had to be evicted with the door closed. Undaunted, I left the door open the following night, determined if necessary to stay awake until daylight. This noble project turned out to be impracticable, as I found I was nodding over my book in a matter of minutes.

I was determined, and I must admit, truly terrified. My own safety was not threatened, but I did not want the cats to kill each other. Without preamble, as I lay pondering the matter, a thought came to me: "If *I* don't believe we can all sleep safely together, *they* won't believe it either. I'm keeping this battle going by my own fear."

I heard my heart thumping as I tried desperately to clear my mind of doubt, saying over and over to myself, "It will be perfectly O.K. It will be perfectly O.K. It will be perfectly O.K."–until I believed it, or had convinced myself that I believed it to the point at which exhaustion took over and I fell asleep. When I awoke in the morning, three cats were peacefully snoozing on my bed. They have been with me there every night since, except for a couple of nights immediately after the inevitable setback.

It had taken two months of patiently putting the program

into effect before what I considered the final capitulation, when the open-door policy was put in operation on a twenty-four-hour basis. All had been well for three weeks, and I felt like a well-qualified lion tamer. The only time I closed the door was when I served Minnie's breakfast in the bedroom. (She never took advantage of the open door to escape confinement.) I thought she was entitled to privacy when breakfast time arrived and that she would digest her first bites better. (One of Jo-Jo's friendly gestures is to eat from Minnie's dishes, which does not disturb her provided she has had a taste first.) I would not say that Minnie was divinely happy about having visits from the other cats, but at least the rest of us were, and she became increasingly tolerant.

How it happened I will never know. As heavily as I sleep, I dream vividly; somewhere in my dreams one night I seemed to hear a raucous caterwauling, to which I seemed to add something loud enough to be heard above the uproar and horrendous enough to put the fear of Madam into any cat within hearing distance. At any rate, whether there was such a cat discussion during the night or not, there were no signs of battle in the morning—no blobs of fur torn out by angry claws—and I assumed that Minnie was under the bed when I awoke and did not see her. Jo-Jo and SuziTu were peacefully sleeping on the covers.

With all the alertness of a hibernating bear in midwinter, I lumbered out to the kitchen to go through the usual feeding routines for all of us. Jo-Jo immediately began trying to climb the walls, pointing eagerly up and reaching as high as possible toward the ceiling, chattering a blue streak. It took me a while to register anything more than feeble curiosity, but finally I followed his glance to the top of the dish cupboards and looked into Minnie's golden eyes. She was reposing peacefully, unruffled and apparently content, in one of her favorite prewar haunts.

Sure, I had invited her to join us all, to leave her self-imposed confinement and live a normal life again. But so suddenly, so high up, and in the *morning*—no!

With my coffee came another horrible thought and real panic. Minnie had returned to her old favorite home to die. I was certain of it. Spilling coffee, I flew out to the kitchen to look at her again. She lay there so quietly, only fifteen inches below the ceiling, giving me such sweetly sad smiles that I was convinced she would never come down. Already in a highly excited state over other matters that had nothing to do with cats, I did not need this complication. I begged her to live happily and healthfully for a long, long time—at least until next week. This, I assured her, was no time to leave us. Please, just wait a bit, and we will see if we can do something for you.

She smiled her sweetest and saddest and acted very last-leggish. Again and again during that day, I climbed up on the step-stool to pet her sleek head, to place her food dishes and litter box where she could get at them easily, and to be certain that she was breathing, if her eyes were closed and I heard no familiar snores. Once during the day, she plunked heavily down from the cabinet top to the refrigerator top to the counter below, and ignoring her litter box above, piddled in the sink. Jo-Jo sniffed in distaste, but I did not reprimand her as I scoured the basin. Minnie climbed out of the sink and took up residence on the counter top, apparently too weary and weak to return to her perch. But later, I found her once more on top of the cabinet.

She declined my invitation to come to bed that night, even though I promised to close the door in the faces of the other cats. She complained when I tried to pick her up and said her stomach hurt. I wondered if she would live through the night. She did, and continued her martyred occupation throughout the next morning and half the afternoon. Then suddenly, plunk-plunk-plunk, as agile as an elderly kitten can be, she came down from her perch and without a pause galloped through the living room and hall to her corner in the bedroom. There she sat down and grinned at me. I raced back to the kitchen for her feeding dishes and litter box, intent on giving the best of service, but wishing she would carry her own luggage when she moved without warning.

I issued no further invitations for her to scare me *that* way again; presently, we all could sleep together as before. But there was one evening shortly after her return to the bedroom when she may have evened the score with Jo-Jo. I had been out for a while, and on my return, I found a dozen small nips of Jo-Jo-colored fur around her chair. There was no other indication of battle, and everyone was peacefully snoozing.

Although we can influence each other's minds, *nobody* can change emotional reactions except the emoter himself. If Minnie feels antagonistic toward the other cats, nothing I can do will *make* her like them. Suzi, I am sure, would prefer not to have to share Jo-Jo's love with another female, even an old mother-in-law, but she is warily willing to make an effort and be pleasant to Minnie—avoiding her whenever possible. After all, Minnie is old and crotchety, and Suzi is secure in her knowledge of Jo-Jo's love. So why don't you, I asked myself, just leave well enough alone, and keep Minnie from active battle? Really, they could kill her, if they wanted to. She's too old to stand up and fight for fun.

Was I perhaps tampering too much with my cats? Experimenting with their minds and their ability to make me understand what they want me to understand seemed, initially, like an intriguing, high-minded, humanitarian, and harmless thing to do. Now that I was deeply involved in it, I wondered if perhaps I should not have had some specific preparation for it, other than loving them extravagantly and wanting intensely to understand and—let's face it—influence them.

Imposing the human will on cats is not the key to solving a feud or taming a shrew. Rather, it may be more to the point to discover what the cat really wants and to help him accomplish it or want something better, much as a psychiatrist tries to help the human. Naturally, one cannot allow cats to do *everything* they may want to do, but if they are convinced that their people are aiming at happy coexistence and have a sound approach to it, they will be exceedingly cooperative.

Bribery is unfair. I never offer tidbits in exchange for something I want the cats to do. This is reportedly the technique used by trainers for "animal acts" and cats who work in the entertainment field, but I consider it absolutely cruel. Instead, I use the same distraction technique that works so well with small children. "Jo-Jo, Suzi wants you," will often persuade Jo-Jo out of Minnie's reach when Minnie wants to be left alone. So summoned, Jo-Jo yawns elaborately, gives Minnie one more leave-taking glance, and saunters back to the waiting Suzi, who really *does* want him and is very patiently putting up with his eternal crush on old Minnie.

Complimenting them on their good behavior produces better results than scolding them for their transgressions. I seldom say, "You're a *bad cat*," but whenever necessary I tell them, "That's not a good thing to do." When I must remove Jo-Jo from Minnie's bailiwick, I pick him up firmly but gently, stroke him as I carry him away, and set him down beside SuziTu. I compliment him for spending so much time with Minnie, and tell him that I am pleased with him. There is no need, as I see it, to rave and rant noisily at the way cats behave either toward each other or toward me. In respect to their attitude toward me, it has been a long, long time since any of my little family has willfully done anything to displease me. Of course, they like to tease, but only as long as I enjoy being teased. They want to please because they know I love them.

There are people, however, who don't love cats. They register varying degrees of dislike for various reasons.

Those people who are willfully cruel to animals are capable of being equally violent toward other people. So anyone who finds it necessary to protect a cat from the insanity of a truly vicious person should also be thoroughly wary of that individual's attitude and intent toward humans. I have known (definitely past tense) one or two people who told me in vivid terms what they would do to a cat who raised a paw to them. These are sick people, and since I am not a psychiatrist, I prefer to leave these people strictly alone, preferably in the safe care of professionals.

In the more nebulous regions of ailurophobia (fancy name for cat-hating) are those people, either crassly selfish and willfully cruel or just ignorant and self-centered, who try to impose their wills on cats to make them do tricks. Perhaps the "cat-act" people of the enterainment field would sometimes, but not always, fall into this category. There are relatively few such entertainments in the small-cat or domestic-cat field, but circus acts often include lions and tigers doing stunts for and with their trainers. One reads stories of these big cats dying of heartbreak when they have to retire from their work because of old age, either the animal's or the trainer's. Yet one also reads that some trainers gain cooperation by withholding food until the animal has been forced to learn his trick. A cat who works for love is a happy cat, but a trainer who uses cruelty as his control is beyond the pale.

People who use cats for laboratory experiments fall into both the "good man" and the "bad man" categories, too. In recent years, it has been discovered, to my regret, that the cat's nervous system is sufficiently similar to that of the human to make cats the best subjects for testing certain drugs. But before this discovery was made, I know that stray cats by the dozen were heartlessly confiscated by hospital interns merely because they were easy to find. In either case, the cats on whom the medics work are truly working cats and make a contribution far more significant than that of cats whose job is only to be companions. Cats will charitably forgive ignorance and dumbness in communication if they know that the human intent is good. And they so very much want to earn their keep that those who do this type of work must feel that their lives are well spent. Nevertheless, I wish there were more understanding of the cats who are chosen for physical experiment, so that if they do not want to do it, they could have a choice in the matter and be able to express it.

These divergent groups of cat-haters (or non-cat-lovers) are not to be classified with those other unfortunate humans who are terrified by cats and therefore claim to hate them; nor with those who prefer dogs, and express the dog preference in terms of "I hate cats."

There are some people who are physically allergic to cat fur. It makes them sneeze, their eyes tear, their sinuses clog, and sometimes they break out in hives. If these unfortunate people really love cats enough to be unhappy without them, it is possible to take desensitizing shots to alleviate the allergy. But often it is simply easier to avoid cats like the plague, and when the allergic person feels this way, cats may be either the cause or the effect of the allergy. A bad experience buried in the subconscious mind is often behind the physical reaction.

I have often wondered if there is a connection between people's opinions of themselves and their attitudes toward cats. I suspect that many an ailurophobe hates cats only because he feels that they are better people than he is—more honest, more secure, more loved, more whatever he is not.

I respect a cat's privilege of choosing the people he likes, and seldom have I found one who would be deliberately rude to a human who honestly loves and respects cats. Aloof, yes; but not actually rude. Many people who have thought they hated cats get won over to the other side, thanks to the blandishments of some enterprising cat who insisted on making an issue of it. Cats always know whether people like or dislike them. They do not always care enough to do anything about it. I am not sure whether it is the cat who is most loved or the one who most needs to be loved who sets out to convert the cat-hater. Perhaps, too, the cat sometimes decides that here is an unfortunate human who is really worth saving, when another may not be. Cats are wonderful missionaries, but always ruthlessly discriminating. Just let someone enter the picture with fear or hatred of cats in his heart, and the cat goes into action! With well-programmed teasing malice (or is it because he so wants to be loved?) a cat will make a nuisance of himself by swarming all over the antagonistic person.

One day during census-taking time, an unknown lady rang my doorbell and asked to come in to ask questions. I sat her on my sofa, where she immediately cringed into the corner as though she would like to lean right back through the wall and disappear. She had seen Suzanne and Joey, and they had seen her.

Together, they ran up to her, jumped into her lap, and climbed up to her neck, where they tucked damp noses under her trembling chin. Stupidly, I thought they were overwhelmed with recognition of a true cat-lover—until I noticed the pallor of the woman's face. After I peeled the cats off her chest, she asked only the briefest questions for her census report and beat a hasty retreat. The poor woman must have been as terrified of cats as is my friend Blanche, and they grinningly, maliciously, deliberately badgered her.

There are no neutral people-reactions to cats. The cat-lover really loves cats. The cat-hater cannot stand them. Both are uncompromising. Most people who do not like cats simply do not know them. There are several reasons: Blanche, who has always been terrified by even the sight of a cat, is convinced it has some deep-rooted psychiatric cause and regretfully has to live with her terror. (So do her cat-possessed friends and their cats.)

Poor Blanche—and poor Alice! Alice lived all her ten years with Blanche's closest friends, who happen also to be neighbors. Only a couple of apartment houses separate them, so Blanche was a frequent visitor. But through all those ten years of Alice's life, Blanche could not stay in the same room with any cat. So often was Alice banished by "here comes Blanche" that these words alone came to produce the desired reaction. "Here cames Blanche" usually sent Alice resignedly out of sight—sometimes inconspicuously under a chair where Blanche would overlook her, sometimes in another room.

Alice was very patient. Obviously, she took no offense at Blanche's revulsion, because Alice understood that there was nothing personal in it. The inner communication between animals and animal lovers, in which I put tremendous faith, must be at work even between animals and people who do not love them. Otherwise, Alice could have made Blanche's life miserable by dogging her footsteps and insisting on making her presence known.

Cat-haters without physical symptoms of allergy can cure themselves, if they want to, merely by opening their minds to the fascinations of a cat, by learning to understand why the cat does what he does. In the process, they will learn something about humans, too. But the willingness to love and understand must be extra strong in order to overcome the antagonism.

2

How To Find Your Cat

Naturally, I would never try to persuade a cat-hater to adopt a cat. It would make them both unhappy. On the other hand, I have given many a sales pitch to people who thought that, for one reason or another, they could not or should not have a cat, although they loved them.

Cats are now rated a close second (presumably to dogs) in popularity as house pets. There are millions of them living happily with people, and although they are generally expected to live no more than ten or twelve years, it is not unheard of for a cat to live to be thirty-four if he is properly understood, physically cared for, and loved. So a cat can be a long-term companion.

Although there are restrictive clauses in many city-apartment leases against pets in general and dogs in particular, cats are usually an exception. So they are ideal companions for people with well-supervised, not-too-young children, or for people who love all animals and want one to talk to because they live alone.

Inviting a cat to share your home entails some degree of responsibility. Cats should never be taken into a home in which the children need a substitute for a mother or are bored with their mechanized toys. Nor can the vacationing family justify leaving a cat behind them when they migrate at the end of the holiday, just because "he came to us and we fed him, but we have no room for him in the city." Once you have allowed a cat to feel that home is where you are, you have accepted responsibility. He has become as much a member of your family as a child and is equally dependent on you. You cannot toss him out to fend for himself, as he may have been doing when he adopted you. Should you find yourself unable to keep a cat who depends on you, take him to the nearest ASPCA or animal shelter, so that he has a chance of finding a permanent home.

How old a child should be when he has his first pet depends on the child's ability to understand the pet's needs for rest, privacy, and gentleness. My eight-year-old grandson has more or less grown up with my cats. They loved and watched over him as a baby, even as his mother and I watched *him* to be sure that he would not maul the cats. Shortly after his eighth birthday, his mother asked the familiar question: "Where can I find two kittens?"

There are many ways of finding a cat who wants to live with you. Vaguely, I remember Brownie, who was literally the answer to a little girl's insistence. I had met a litter of new kittens on my way home from school, and the neighbor who sponsored them was delighted to find a home for one. In the country, there are always kittens to be found just for the asking.

Domino joined the family in a rather different way. My husband was teaching school in a small town near Buffalo, New York, that year, and one evening we decided to drive into the next town for a hamburger just to break the routine. As we parked the car, a tiny black kitten with white chin and paws came galloping up to us as though he had been waiting for hours and was *so* glad we had come at last. We were both pushovers for cats, and this little waif begged urgently to join us. We forgot the hamburgers and took him home.

I am certain he had no home, but I must confess we never gave it a thought (which is one good reason for never putting out your cat at night). It is difficult indeed to have to ignore the plea of any little cat I meet who looks up eagerly and asks, "Don't you want me?" But he may be only temporarily lost or unsatisfied with his perfectly good home. I still feel a bit guilty about the possibility that we kidnaped Domino and left someone bereft of a very sweet kitten.

Acquiring Brownie and Domino were rather haphazard and informal processes not to be wholeheartedly recommended. And the ways in which both Monster and Minstrel came to live with us were almost as haphazard.

When my daughter Anne was nine years old, we were prowling around Greenwich Village one evening and happened to pass a cat-adoption center. We both went into tailspins of ecstasy over the kittens in the window of the closed shop and went home to seriously consider whether or not Anne was old enough to take responsibility for a pet.

As a working mother, by then without a partner in parenthood, I had developed early the habit of discussing things seriously with Anne, encouraging her to share as much responsibility as she could accept. We decided that a cat was in order, and I gleefully announced to all my friends and office acquaintances that we were in the market for a kitten.

For a while, it looked as though we might end up with a whole menagerie of kittens. Everyone seemed to know of kittens that were available for adoption. It finally boiled down to two domestic short-haireds who were described as equally adorable, one white with black markings, the other black with white trim. Anne and I decided on the white one, not having seen either, but putting our trust in the friend who recommended them.

"Oh, look at the little monster!" I exclaimed happily as my friend brought out the seven-week-old kitten from the folds of her scarf. Thus, Monster joined our family.

When Monnie was a year and a half old, neutered and well-established in our home, Minnie joined us. For two nights in succession, I had heard what sounded like a kitten in the outer hall of our apartment house, but although I had searched my own hall and the ones above and below, I could not find it. Since I have never been able to bear the sound of a lost child or a lost animal, my maternal instinct was thoroughly aroused. Nevertheless, I had to give up my fruitless search on the second evening. The next morning, just after Anne had left for school, I was about to settle down to work when once again I heard the kitten sound in the hallway. This time I found her—crouched, frightened and lonely and small—against the elevator door.

I invited her in, thinking she was shut out of someone else's apartment. She was a little black cat, probably about six months old, although she may have been a bit older, since within a few days it was obvious that she was in heat. At any rate, I offered her a meal, and she ate as though food were going out of style while Monnie glared suspiciously at her from a safe-but-pounceable distance.

Warily, I trailed the procession around the little apartment as the black kitten, her appetite temporarily appeased, investigated every nook and corner, followed by Monster, slinking low against the floor and stopping short every time she turned her frightened gold-green eyes over her shoulder at him. At last she discovered the bathroom, where his litter box was located, and this was the last straw for the lord of the manor. He gathered his legs under him, bared his teeth, and prepared to make hash of the invader of his privacy.

"Monster!" I cried, horrified lest he should attack her. "Let the lady go!" Startled, he stopped in his tracks and stared at me over his hunched shoulder. He was still in low-slung readiness for pouncing, which gave him an amusingly furtive look. Slowly, he turned and looked back at the newcomer, who was intent on doing what she had to do and tidying up afterward. When she emerged, Monster walked up to her and kissed her nose. It had taken two hours to begin a devotion that lasted the remaining dozen years of his life.

Feeling that it was now safe to leave the two cats alone together, I sought out the building superintendent to ask about the little black cat's bereft owners so that I could return her to them.

"Oh," he chuckled. "You have her? She's been out on the street for the last three days, trying to get into this house. You're the only people who have a cat here, so I guess she doesn't belong to anybody." We named her Minstrel.

So that is another way of acquiring a cat.

One friendship that I value very highly started the first moment I met Othello. I had been vacationing with friends at their camp on one of New York's Finger Lakes, and we had returned to their beautiful, old-farmhouse home, back to work on all our schedules for the following day. As soon as we had unloaded the cars and opened the house, the cats began to appear at the back door. Seldom allowed in the house, these cats hold down a good job keeping the mice under control in the out-buildings, and of course we had made provisions for their food before we went away. They were glad to have us back, nevertheless, and we all went out to greet them.

"Oh, there's that black cat," Dottie said worriedly. "He came around a couple of weeks ago, I don't know where from, and I'm afraid of him."

The black cat was indeed an imposing sight. Long-haired, his coat rough and full of burrs, he stared out of enormous copper-colored eyes and proclaimed—in a loud Siamese voice, used at this moment as though he had not spoken to anyone in days and wanted to make up for lost time.

I replied in Siamese-cat imitation and walked toward him with my hand out. "Look out!" Dottie warned. "He's a wild one!" I squatted before the big black cat, talking softly in his language and listening to his happy response. In less than a minute, this allegedly dangerous beast was rolling over and over, licking my hand, rubbing against my ankles, purring like a well-tuned motor.

"There's nothing wrong with this cat that a good brushing won't take care of," I told Dottie. "Except that he's been terribly lonely, and he wants to be loved." The cat looked at me with limpid eyes, pathetically happy to be understood, and we have been close friends ever since. In fact, a few months later I made another visit to his new home. As I drove in and stopped the car, I found him eager to greet me, wearing a grin of delight, his long fur carefully brushed. Dottie said he had been restlessly pacing all day and that he obviously knew I was coming.

Dottie's husband and I had named him Othello when we

had persuaded Dottie to allow him to stay with them. He appeared to approve of the title and to give all his loyalty to his new people. A most gentlemanly cat, he is one of the very few that Dottie allows in her house. Since he is a truly beautiful animal, he is frequently in such demand when guests come that he can show off, which he loves to do. When I am there, it is my delightful chore to round him up when his presence is desired.

Dottie says, "Winnie, get Othello." I go to the door, bellow into the forty acres twice—"Othello! Waa-ow! Othello! Waa-ow!"—and close the door if it is wintry weather.

"Where's the cat?" Dottie wants to know.

"He'll be here in two minutes," I tell her confidently. Two minutes later, I open the door and let Othello come in, waving his magnificent plume, pleased to be invited, and politely inquiring if we have any liver for him. No one in the community seems to have any knowledge of Othello's background or origins. He was a full-grown cat, house-trained, and people-oriented when he decided to move into his new home. He took over with an air of authority and chased the other cats up trees as though he had always owned them. Yet he has never made a pass at toddling visitors or guest dogs.

He is delighted at the opportunity to sit on a lap, and although we friends spend a great deal of our indoor time sitting around the table in the comfortable old kitchen, it apparently never occurs to him to investigate the table top. Othello is a noble cat indeed, one whom I am proud to number among my next-of-kin felines, even though I see him no more than three or four times a year. We think he may have been abandoned, dropped off by the roadside from a car, so we are extra-loving to him to make up for the mistreatment to which he may have been exposed.

* * *

Ever since Minnie's arrival, I had been preaching to all my one-cat friends, "You've simply *got* to have *two* cats! It's so much easier than having just one." And it is. They keep each other company, and although they want human love and companionship, too, they do not make nuisances of themselves about it.

Nevertheless, living in a city apartment, I would never have thought of having *more* than two cats at a time, had it not been for the fact that when Monnie died, he was thirteen years old. I was well aware that Minnie, no more than a year younger, could not be expected to live much longer. (Little did I know that she would be hale and hearty at eighteen!)

In her loneliness for Monster, Minnie became demanding. She was underfoot all the time, weaving around my ankles, never wanting me out of her sight. All the love and apparently helpless dependence she had given to Monster for a dozen years was suddenly directed at me. She was a pathetic little black widow, lost without her mate. But she wasn't going to die of grief; she was going to have her Madam's attention now all to herself. Perhaps for the first time, I became aware of Minnie then as a personality, instead of as Monnie's shadow.

It was obvious that I must find another cat to keep her company, and in view of her old age, it seemed logical to look for two kittens of the same age so that they could grow up happily together. This time, I called Dr. Roth, my veterinarian, to ask his advice on the best source of kittens.

"You need to find kittens that are born in love, in somebody's kitchen," he said. "I have a client who's always having kittens. You might try her first, and if she can't help you, I'll see what else I can find." Cat doctors almost always have a list of people who want either kittens or homes for kittens.

I phoned the lady Dr. Roth had suggested, and indeed she

did have a new litter, still so young they could not leave their mother. I made a date to check with her in another month and tried to wait patiently. The prospect was quite exciting because the lady had told me that these kittens were half-Siamese. Although I had never had a Siamese give me more than a passing cross-eyed glance, I knew they were not only beautiful to look at, but were also reputed to be exciting companions. We had agreed that since they were only half-Siamese, I would pay her half of her usual charge for full-bred Siamese; but I was a bit baffled by her reference to "the white one" and "the others." So I discussed the coming event with my neighbor, whose sister raises Siamese cats.

"Oh," Judy assured me, "you know, half-Siamese are *always* black. They never look the least bit like Siamese cats, but they're sometimes more fun than the pure-breds." I was a trifle disappointed that they were not going to look like the beautiful, exotic creatures I had envisioned, but kittens are kittens, and I love them all. It was still a delightful prospect, and I spent the waiting time assuring Minnie that she was going to like her new little friends. Minnie seemed less than impressed and continued to follow me around the house.

At long last, the appointed day arrived, and I went to pick out two kittens from the litter of three. Sure enough, one was white and had the beginnings of little slate-gray markings on nose, tail, and paws, and bright blue eyes just like her handsome Siamese father's. The other two babies were glossy black with twinkling golden eyes. Their mother was a gray tabby. It was a toss-up between the little black ones, since their owner assured me all three were females, so I chose the one who came to me first and of course took the little charmer with the Oriental look.

I named the blonde one "Josephine" and the black one

"Suzanne." But it was no more than a day or two of constantly calling each by the other's name before I said, "I'm sure I've got them reversed. The blonde one is much more a Suzanne type—and besides, I'm willing to bet the black one should be called Josephus."

My instinct proved correct. As they grew up, it became obvious that Josephus was going to be a handsome black tom, and Suzanne became more feminine every day. What was most remarkable was that Suzanne could have won a prize as a thoroughbred Siamese in any cat show. Judy was astounded when I showed the kittens to her. She researched the matter and came back with an authoritative edict that once in 10,000 times a half-breed Siamese of the first generation looks like a thoroughbred.

It was the intriguing differences between Joey and his sister, in both appearance and personality—little black Joe so outgoing and beautiful Suzanne so shy and timid—that first made me determine to raise kittens. Researching the subject of inbreeding, I read that although it should not be overdone (a litter or two from brother and sister should be the limit), it would not harm either them or their kittens. I had never had a litter of kittens to gladden my heart and fill in my education, and I could think of nothing that would be more delightful. Furthermore, I was intrigued by the genetics that had produced Suzanne, so completely Siamese in all respects. Would the Siamese characteristics prove stronger than the tabby heritage in Susie's kittens?

So I decided not to have either Joey or Susie altered. In due course, they matured and mated, but failed to reproduce. One or both of them may have been naturally sterile. I was disappointed and hoped that the next time Susie wanted to mate she might have better luck. Meanwhile, there was nothing I could do about it, and I consoled myself with the thought that having kittens in an apartment did sound like rather a vast project.

Then Joey died, and I knew that without too much delay I must find a male kitten, a full-bred Siamese, to keep Susie happy.

At that time, I subscribed to my Connecticut home-town newspaper, which almost never reached my mailbox until Monday, although it is published on Thursday each week. Accordingly, when the paper turned up in Friday's mail, I just knew there was something special for me in that issue. I opened it immediately to the "Pets for Sale" column, and there it was: the first "Siamese-kittens-for-sale" ad in four weeks! (Born in love, in somebody's kitchen, just as the doctor ordered, too.)

I phoned for an appointment, and on Valentine's Day I met and purchased two-month-old Chieng Jo-Jo, son of Chieng Ho-Ho and Chieng Leing, complete with impressive pedigree and several show champions in his background. I paid what seemed a high price for him, but rationalized it by figuring I could get it back by eventually mating him with a full Siamese and producing kittens that would make up the cost.

Chieng Jo-Jo is a prince among cats—sweet of disposition, loving without being maudlin about it, fantastically handsome, and very self-effacing except when he wants immediate love. At such times, he dances anxiously around my feet, looking up with a most appealing urgency in his bright blue eyes, quietly asking "Waa-aa?" And I must then pick him up, hold him close, kiss the top of his head, and put him down again on the floor as soon as he begins to struggle, which is very soon indeed. A little love goes a long way with Jo-Jo.

Suzanne, then a year and a half old, recognized his masculine potential at once and waited patiently for him to mature. Minstrel, whom I suspect lives so long just to see what will happen next, took him in stride and eventually decided he was her own idea. He loved her as his mother, and for a long time she relished his deferential attention.

But just at the time when Jo-Jo was old enough to reward Susie's patience, Susie died very suddenly. Jo-Jo refused to eat. He moped sadly about the house, devastated by his loss, pitifully appealing to both Minnie and me for extra reassurance and love. He grew thin. His tail hung low, and he no longer danced.

Elsie, who came to clean once a week or to cat-sit daily when I was away, heckled me. "Mrs. Carrie," she said, "if you don't get another cat pretty soon, that Jo-Jo going to die." I took another look at his sad, woebegone little face and once again opened the home-town newspaper directly to the "Pets for Sale" column. Two days later, I took SuziTu back to the city to live with Jo-Jo, Minnie, and me.

Jo-Jo examined the two-and-a-half-month-old kitten thoughtfully and thoroughly. He sat down and stared at her for a long moment, and I saw his eyes change from that haunted, sad dullness of bereavement to their normal bright blue. Jo-Jo loved SuziTu from the first time they met, and as patiently as Suzanne had waited for him to mature, he waited for Suzi.

As Suzi grew up to teen-age cathood, she flirted and taunted Jo-Jo unmercifully. A thoroughbred Siamese, she was as feminine as a beauty queen and as heartless in her teasing. Poor Jo-Jo, mature and adoring her, tried to take out his frustrations on old Minnie, who slapped his face and snarled. So Jo-Jo waited, his eyes full of patient longing.

Finally, Suzi decided she had had enough of girlish flirtations and was ready to start raising a family. Jo-Jo, always the gentleman and mindful of Minnie's rebuffs, was slow and cautious in his response. Howling importunities and imprecations, Suzi rolled in anguished desire. When at last all was quiet after a particularly harrowing session between them, I sketched my sleeping pair, who were clasped in each other's paws as only cats can arrange themselves, apparently content. Nevertheless, I had no definite clue as to whether or not I could start counting kittens. After all, Joey and Suzanne had failed to produce any. This time, however, I had better luck.

One other source of supply, especially for fancy breeds but also for ordinary domestic short-haireds, is cat shows. I have never entered my cats in shows and cannot speak from experience on the subject. But I understand that some cats, and a lot of people, find cat shows entertaining, rewarding, and instructive. Furthermore, even though not all the cats entered in the contests are for sale, the cat show is the place where you will meet cat fanciers and breeders, in both the amateur and professional groups, who can steer you to just the kittens you want.

The shows are sponsored by the various cat societies, such as the Cat Fanciers' Association and the Cat Fanciers' Federation, both of which register feline pedigrees. They have various classes in which cats can be entered for show purposes, including classes for cats that are not members of a fancy breed. The local newspaper's pet columnist or your veterinarian can tell you how to contact these associations for up-to-date information and probably give you the dates and place of the next show in your area.

Perhaps the most deserving and appreciative cat possessors may be found without cost at the cat-adoption centers—the ASPCA, the privately endowed animal shelters such as Bide-

A-Wee in New York City, or through the file maintained by the American Feline Society, which has many branches throughout the country. This turned out to be the solution for my daughter when she was searching for just the two kittens who most wanted to live with her family.

Obviously, there are many ways in which you can locate a cat to live with you. But whatever method you choose, these are the indications of good health that you should be careful to look for before you take your kitten home:

Check his eyes to be sure they are bright and clear. Check his nose to be sure it is not running. Check his ears for cleanliness and speak to him to be certain he can hear. Search his coat for fleas and be sure he has none. Watch him play for a while so you will know that he moves with normal agility. Ask if he has had his shots yet, and if not, what arrangements can be made and what would be the proper timing. And of utmost importance, sit quietly with him for a while to be sure that you and he really like each other.

3

The Personality Kids

Since my early childhood, nine cats have called me their own, and I have been on a next-of-kin basis with at least a half-dozen others. I have nodding acquaintance with still more and try my best to keep aloof from cats I meet by the wayside, lest they decide to follow me. Not one of the cats I have known has failed to have a personality completely distinct from each of the others.

Of course at times they have similar traits, interests, and reactions. But shy Suzanne was as different from mischievous SuziTu as joyous, outgoing Josephus was from reticent, self-effacing Jo-Jo. Sweet Minnie and the ever-dignified Monster, with their apparently diverse extremes of intelligence, could never be said to remind me (except by being cats, too) of self-sufficient Mowser, bossy Alice, snooty Queenie, or puppyish Domino.

Then there were the kittens, one from each of SuziTu's litters—Jennie, who was a lone wolf, and Mr. X, who was a me-tooer—both of whom left big gaps when I had to part with them.

It was not only in appearance that Suzanne and Josephus, her brother, differed. Suzanne was extremely shy, easily frightened, and very demanding when she wanted to be loved. "Love me *now!*" is a typical Siamese exhortation and brooks no argument. She was exceedingly beautiful, very graceful, and agile, and she had the most raucous voice I have ever heard from a cat. Siamese, I decided, are so magnificent to look at and so charming to know that they simply have to have horrible voices just to keep them from being too perfect. But *her* voice was rather overdoing it.

I felt I had retaliated a bit when I scribbled:

Slender breath of pastel fur and fragile bone,
Sable-masked and tipped on tail and ears and toes,
Sky-blue saucers lighting heart-shaped face—
Disposition matching, filled with charm and grace—
Beauty is Suzanne
From Siam.

Tiny feet scarce touch the floor (or chair or couch).
Swift, seductive, feline, female, coy, and shy,
Well-behaved, and loving as a cat can be—
So demure, petite, and soft upon my knee!
But the way she *talks*—
All in squawks!

From her tiny pointed jaws there comes such noise
Bellow of a cow in pain would softer be!
These horrendous sounds that issue forth may mean

Joy, frustration, hunger, love, or "I'm a queen!"
Constant chatter, cease!
Siamese!!!

But how gladly I would have put up with this one small imperfection if she could have lived her normal life span!

Her brother Joey, on the other hand, was blithely frank about being a commoner. He made no pretense at Siamese agility or beauty or voice. He was a laughing, loving, romping, little black cat without a fault that I could discover. Elsie, on her weekly visits to clean the apartment, kept asking me which of the three—Minnie, Joey, or Susie—was my favorite. I never admitted favoritism, lest I should hurt someone's feelings even by *thinking* favoritism. But when Joey died, I did admit that I had loved him best of all. He was so abandoned in happiness that I sometimes called him "Joy." He was truly joy personified:

Burn brightly, fire.
Reflect my Joey's amber eyes
That never saw you, never will.
Burn brightly, like his joyous heart,
Too soon still.

Walk lightly, ghost
Of Joey. Not a common cat,
My Joe was joy in feline guise—
With purr, with jaunty gait, with voice,
With bright eyes.

Cling tightly, heart,
To mem'ries cherished, all too short—
Of love and play and strut and howl,

Soft paws and glossy coat like coal,
Prance and prowl.

Sing nightly, Sue
And Minnie. Joey's gone from here,
But somewhere now a kitten's born
With Joey's joyous spirit. Sing!
Do not mourn.

Of course, the differences between Joey and Suzanne were perhaps more noticeable to me because they were siblings. Jo-Jo and SuziTu, on the other hand—and Minnie and Monnie—coming from different families, would naturally be expected to have different personalities. But the mental and physical attitude of a female also differ from those of a male cat.

Both Minnie and SuziTu have always shown an extremely feminine interest in male cats. Sometimes it is a husband-hunting interest; sometimes it is "this is my pride-and-joy son." Minnie, as long as Monster was alive, was so subservient and subordinated to his strong personality that I thought of her as almost feeble-minded. She was comically dependent on Monster. She never did *anything* without first giving him a deferential, questioning look, asking for permission. It was not until he died that she began to come into her own and to take off the housewife's apron that I always mentally saw on her. The change was rapid, and by the time we had waited out the arrival of Josephus and Suzanne, Minnie had begun to be a matriarch, gowned in sleek black satin, a bit overweight as well as overbearing, and definitely a personality to be reckoned with in the household.

Little Joey's outgoing disposition very quickly won Minnie's affection, and perhaps his physical resemblance to her was apparent to her, too. He looked so much like her that he could have been passed off as her own kitten. For whatever reason, Minnie took Joey in charge and mothered him a month after Monster died, although she gave Suzanne nothing more than politeness. (Again, when Jo-Jo came to live with us, it was only three days before Minnie was mothering *him* and starting to bring him up in the way she wanted a youngster to grow.)

She seemed to take special pride in Joey as he grew into a handsome black tom, but in his kittenish boisterousness, he got away with undreamed-of pranks and familiarities, while Minnie smiled, scolded, cuffed, and kissed him as her maternal instinct commanded. Like a maiden aunt suddenly blessed with a child to care for, all her motherliness came to the fore for Joey.

There was never such closeness between Minnie and either Suzanne or SuziTu. And the female kittens apparently could not care less, for although they never made an effort to antagonize the old lady, neither did they tease or cajole her into play or outraged anger, as did the male kittens. With purposefully feminine hip-swinging designed to attract the boys away from their foster mother, they paraded past old Minnie as though she were a statue—to be saluted if necessary, but avoided if possible.

Very different from Monster is Jo-Jo, yet SuziTu's attitude toward him is reminiscent of Minnie's toward her beloved Monnie. Reminiscent only, for SuziTu seems to feel much more equal than subservient to Jo-Jo. They share; Minnie asked permission and approval. SuziTu loves Jo-Jo and shows it in her feminine flirtations and gentle little teasings, as well as in her loyalty when sides must be chosen. Often I find the two of them lying on a comfortable chair, heads together, paws entwined, looking like a two-headed bundle of soft fur. Sometimes, one will wake from the joint nap and begin to lick the other's face, and then they arrange their heads so that they can lick each other simultaneously.

But Jo-Jo does not dominate SuziTu as Monnie dominated Minnie. Jo-Jo is neither a dominating personality nor as teasingly gay as SuziTu. Even as a baby, his little face always wore a solemn look that has turned out to be a habitual expression. Part of it is that his front fangs are too long to be contained easily in his face when his lips are closed. His very blue eyes are usually roundly wide open, even when he suddenly breaks into a gleeful gallop and goes tearing exuberantly around the house from the sheer joy of being alive. Jo-Jo is inclined to be sedately deferential to me, anstead of a dignified equal as Monster was. He is unerringly polite to me and to SuziTu, but never fawning. When he wants something, he asks for it quietly but firmly, no self-pity in his voice, but an anxious urgency in his eyes and sometimes an eagerly upraised, tentatively drooping forepaw for added appeal. His only outward rudeness is toward Minnie, whom he bedevils with a wicked gleam in his eyes and a cautious, wary slink in his body attitude as he approaches her.

And the change in a cat's personality and attitudes, physical and emotional, as old age approaches is another interesting thing to watch. The Minnie who used to be afraid of her shadow, who used to run at the sound of the doorbell, has turned into a self-confident, irascible, dominating dowager. She likes to have people stroke her head, but when she has had enough, she reaches out with a firm, claw-tipped paw to put a stop to it. Sometimes in the middle of contented purring, she suddenly bares her teeth and emits a guttural word of alarming profanity, only to resume the purring.

She is remarkably agile, despite her age, but she is flat-footed. Instead of walking on her forepaw toes as she used to, she walks on the entire forepaw, as though she were wearing snowshoes. This gives her vast, unwieldly rump and pendulous abdomen a peculiar elevation and swing. Yet there is great dignity about the old lady, and an enormous alertness and interest in whatever is going on around her. She gives and demands as much affection as a Siamese, and I have changed my mind about her being a nitwit. Her understanding and sympathy, expressed with a loving paw on my cheek, have increased with her age, but I believe they are based on a latent intelligence that just never got expressed while the dominating Monster was around to overshadow her.

As I replaced him in her affection and loyalty, she has gradually assumed his share of the household management, has teamed up with me. Although I often call her "old lady," she knows I intend the term with respect. It makes her grin at me and purr like a sports car.

"Cats are selfish" is a stock complaint from the people who do not know them. "Cats are sneaky, tricky, disloyal, undependable . . ." however they express it, it is another misunderstanding cliché. And occasionally, more realistically close to the truth, "Cats are too independent. They won't obey unless they feel like it."

I would not mind so much if these maligners prefaced their generalities with the word "some"—"*Some* cats are. . . ." There are some people, too, who have undesirable characteristics, just as there are some cats who, through the necessity of looking out for themselves, become apparently selfish, sneaky, or disloyal. But I do not believe that these are necessarily inherent traits. More likely, these cats are misunderstood and neglected. They cannot survive in any other way.

I have never known a cat who was not willing to share with his loved ones—cat or human—or a cat who would not put up a fight for his own. Blind obedience is indeed beneath a cat's extreme sense of dignity, but cheerful cooperation is natural to most cats who are treated with respect, affection, and a sincere attempt at understanding.

Mowser is a prime example of polite give-and-take. He is one of the cats who considers me next of kin, since for five years we lived practically in each other's laps on weekends. He used to come downstairs to my terrace apartment, pass the time of day with me, and ask if I happened to have any milk to spare. (Perversely, he will not drink milk when it is offered by his own family upstairs at his feeding station.)

I almost never gave Mowser anything other than milk, since he is getting along in years and gaining weight enough to be a bit too slow to make a quick get-away from the wild life that surrounds him, should the need arise. But one evening, I had something particularly tasty in the line of scraps from a steak, and I set the plate outside my terrace door. Next morning, the plate was empty except for a dead mouse. Mowser had left me a thank-you gift.

That was not the only one of his gestures of gratitude. When he first came to live with his family, the children were quite young. They both loved him, and he took turns sleeping first with Barbara, then with Harold, to avoid a show of partiality. But Barbara must have been his secret favorite, for it was in her bed that he deposited most of his prizes.

First it was a frog. Then it was a dead snake. Then toads and baby bunnies and birds all came into the house, unharmed but frightened, and always left on Barbara's bed if Mowser could persuade them to stay there until she found them.

He got bawled out for bringing in the dead snake, so he

tried live creatures. He did not get a much better reception with them either, but he continued to try. He hid the baby bunny in a closet, where in terror it thumped its little legs until it was discovered and turned loose outdoors again.

When the frogs did not find a welcome mat in Barb's bedroom, Mowser took to bringing them home late in the fall to spend the winter in the laundry room in a pan of water, placed there to catch a slow drip from the washing machine. When dead mice were given the heave-ho and Mowser was scolded instead of thanked, he gave up trying to catch the live ones that occasionally appear indoors during a cold winter. His intentions were good. He had tried to please and to express appreciation for his home, but humans were indeed difficult.

It was understandable, then, that when Mowser's services were really needed, he declined to live up to the sound of his name. (His name, as a matter of fact, came from his habitual question, "Ma-ow?"). It was Christmastime, and the house was so full of company that an extra mattress had to be imported from the not-quite-useless pile in the children's playhouse.

My first awareness of anything unusual occurring above me was the sound of mad scrambling, squeals, and shrieks of excitement. Investigating to see what I was missing in the Christmas preparations, I discovered a mouse running loose in the house. In fact, there appeared to be two mice. Mowser sat calmly disinterested, occasionally licking a paw and passing it over his expressionless black face, while Barbara, always adept with animals, chased the frightened field mice, caught them in her hands, and at my soft-hearted request, turned them loose outdoors.

But the mice seemed to find a quick way back into the warmth, for they kept scuttling through living room, kitchen, and bedrooms. When the fray was over, we totaled thirteen of the little invaders and tracked them to their nest in the old mattress that had been inviting to them when the browning autumn fields became too cold. At least two families of field mice had obviously been born in the soft stuffing.

Mowser had finally been cajoled into catching *one*, and he looked dubious about the propriety of such an act. Having put a weighty paw on the little rodent, he glanced over his shoulder to see whether he was in for a reprimand or for unaccustomed praise.

In my own cat family, I have seen very few instances of selfishness. When, on rare occasions, I have had a T-bone left from a steak, there have been questions as to which cat should have it first, questions that were decided without more than a growl or two by the one who reached it first. A growl can be a terrible threat when teeth are both bared *and* sunk into a bone. It goes with an appropriately menacing glare delivered above the coveted bone and carries a clear message.

Only the greedy little kittens have ever stooped to stealing out of someone else's dish or making it impossible for another cat to get his share. Time and again, on the other hand, I used to see Minnie wait for Monnie to taste first before she approached her own exactly similar dish; and I have watched Jo-Jo sniff his dinner, lift his head, look expectantly over his shoulder, and wait until SuziTu had joined him before he began to eat.

As to the accusation that cats are sneaky, I firmly believe it is as false as their alleged selfishness. Certainly they are looking out for themselves. The history of cats for centuries has been one of survival of the fittest. But sneaky—no! They are curious about everything unknown. They are cautious until they have made a thorough investigation. So they approach the unknown with slow, tentative movement, not at the gallop that would leave them too vulnerable should trouble be waiting.

As part of this prepared-for-anything attitude, it is especially important for any self-respecting cat to preserve his dignity in the face of whatever may come. Startled during an investigation, a cat may retaliate for even the most fancied injury, and hang his head apologetically afterward when he realizes it was a false alarm. Furthermore, some cats like to tease more than others. This combination of characteristics can, I suppose, readily be mistaken for trickery, but it is a mistake.

Perhaps it is the cat's tendency to brashness that contributes to the "too independent" tag. For my part, I want an animal to be independent. Independence is a relative thing. I think there is more of a sense of privacy than willful defiance when a cat sits calmly with his back to me, refusing to hear me, even though he cannot help the fact that his ears, of their own accord, point back in my direction. There is a sense of play involved, too—the teasing play that is so typical of cats throughout their lives.

Nevertheless, I would be the last to deny that cats place a high value on doing what they wish to do, when they wish to do it, in the way they deem most satisfactory to them. It is this declaration of independence that makes the cat the possessor rather than the possessed, and I admire and sometimes envy him for it.

Monster was the most self-consciously dignified cat I ever knew. If, during a sociable conversation with someone he liked, in which Monster was usually a happy participant, I laughed suddenly, all the delight was instantly wiped from

Monnie's expressive eyes. It was absolutely necessary to tell him, "I'm laughing *with* you, Monnie, not *at* you."

Surprisingly, Monster always accepted this explanation and relaxed. If the explanation were not given, he would turn away and sulk, refusing to participate any longer. On the rare occasions when I actually did laugh at him, even after explaining why, I had to apologize before he would forgive me. He did not share Minnie's ability to accept herself as being occasionally an inadvertent comic.

Monnie's dignity was sometimes a trial to him. He would, for example, never look at his own reflection in a mirror under any circumstances, even if avoidance meant shutting his eyes or turning his face away. This aversion stemmed from his first encounter with his own image.

Curiosity led him to a mirror; there he found an adversary looking at him, a handsome black-and-white tom with big golden eyes, who advanced toward Monnie's nose as Monnie reached forward to sniff. The noses banged together, and the other cat's was hard and cold. Monster was affronted and raised a paw, only to find it meeting the pads of another paw raised toward him at the same time.

Of course the final blow to his dignity came when he saw my reflection behind his own, turned his head over his shoulder toward me, and realized there was a trick to it because I could not help laughing at his bewilderment. He was utterly chagrined by the experience, for it did not take long for him to understand that he had duped himself into being undignified. He had no hesitation about watching someone else in a mirror, but he stubbornly refused to meet his own eyes.

Not being forgiven by Monster could be a fairly regrettable thing, for he was inclined to be vindictive. If he had been wrong, he never attempted to deny it. But when he thought he had been wronged, he plotted and waited until he could take an eye for an eye. During the thirteen years we lived together, I came to know when he was hatching a plot to get even with me and usually made an effort to forestall it with apologies. His punishments often had teeth in them.

One of his favorite punishments for me was to lunge for my ankles as I climbed into bed. He was scrupulously fair about it. It was the *attempt* that counted, and if he failed to make contact, then I had won that round and he did not try again. If he won, it was with claws extended and intent to draw blood. Wicked game that it was, it became one of our rougher indoor sports as well as punishment for my real or fancied transgressions, such as leaving him alone for a weekend.

There was a very obvious difference between sport and punishment. When he meant serious business, there was no smile to light Monnie's eyes, only an impressive gleam of emotion-enlarged black pupils. When we were playing, however roughly, his golden eyes glowed with laughter around pinpoints of slitted black. As I have said, I learned from him that kittens should not be encouraged to play too roughly, lest they grow up to be hoodlums.

Proud and independent as cats are, when they want or need a human, they are the first to admit it. Only sometimes they do not recognize that they have got into a predicament that requires human assistance. Again, Monnie's dignity was sorely injured the time he fell into the john. Soaking wet, he tried to scramble out unaided and fought like a tiger against my help and the towel I wrapped him in to dry his fur.

But on the few occasions when he was not feeling well, my lap was the only place that could possibly please him;

my soothing voice and sincere sympathy were medicine and stimulants.

Minnie in her young days was always docile. When she first came to us, it was obvious that she had lived unhappily in another home or alone on the streets. She must either have escaped in sheer desperation or been thrown out (if she lived with someone), unwanted because she was an ungainly teenager in heat. In any event, she was frightened by every sound, every strange voice, every ring of the doorbell, every sudden move of a hand. She got over it eventually, but it took more than a year of love, understanding, and persuasion before she could bring herself to stay in the room with us if the doorbell rang. Her immediate impulse was to run and hide, scuttling along in a low-slung, self-effacing crouch into the nearest black shadow or the farthest under-furniture corner, casting alarmed glances over her shoulder from her big, round, green-gold eyes.

In the eighteen years of her life, she has had now sufficient reassurance and fighting-back experience to feel completely secure, but it took a lot of overt loving in the beginning to convince her that she was really wanted.

On the other hand, in her typically feline fashion, she was curious and inclined to explore whenever she had an opportunity. Opportunity came several times in her youth when I opened the door to go to the incinerator, or to say good-by to someone. Our apartment then was next to an inner stairway, and Minnie's fleet paws inevitably took her up it. The sound of pursuit drove her higher and higher, made her frantic, and—in those pre-air-conditioning days when doors were open for summer ventilation—into the first gaping doorway.

Nor, having arrived in a strange place did she come to a halt in the open. Like a homing pigeon, she inevitably sought out the bedroom, shot under the bed, and crouched in the most inaccessible corner she could find. This led to many an embarrassing encounter with people who were disinclined to see any humor in a stranger scrounging around under their beds, pleading with a cat that might or might not exist. (She went so fast and was so black that sometimes they had not seen her.)

A cat's persistence in going upward, ever upward, can lead to all sorts of problems for anyone like me, afraid of height. It is perfectly natural, of course. Cats' claws are curved and hooked for secure footing when they are climbing up to escape a more earth-bound enemy. To get back down again is something for which nature failed to give them any special provision, and they must either back down or turn around and jump. So a treed cat really needs a human friend.

I remember well how Domino, who lived with us in a house with no tall trees nearby, made a beeline for the tallest tree every time we took him to Connecticut for a visit. It required an extension ladder and several anguished hours of persuasion to get him down.

Domino was a sweet little cat and seemed to be as loyal as they come. Always watching through the window for the first sight of his people, he was at the door to greet us long before we reached it. When I went away for a weekend, leaving him alone with my husband, he slept on my vacated pillow. Yet finally, he left me flat to live with someone else, and I blamed myself for his departure.

I had returned to the university for graduate work; for companionship, Domino went with me. I took a room on the first floor of a college rooming house, so that Domino, accustomed to going outdoors at will, could come and go through a window. For some reason, he did not like the new living arrangements. It was not more than a week after I had moved into that first-floor room before he disappeared, never to return.

Two years later, after visiting a friend a few blocks from where I had lived during that graduate-school semester, I took a walk. There, sitting on a doorstep, was Domino, looking very much at home. We looked at each other. I am sure he recognized me, but I did not speak to him because at that time I could not offer him anything in exchange for the home he had evidently chosen for himself. Was he disloyal to me? I have never felt so; rather, I must have let him down in one way or another.

Cats just do not leave home without a reason; on the other hand, they do ask the people they live with to take a certain degree of responsibility for their happiness. Above everything else—even food, I believe—a cat wants a sense of security. If he is not made to feel that he really belongs, that this one place is his home and these people are his people, there is no reason why he should be expected to stick around waiting for occasional crumbs or pats on the head.

So it usually seems to be those cats who live more outdoors than indoors that wander from place to place, sometimes returning to a former home after taking up temporary residence elsewhere. More often, I hear of country cats disappearing and reappearing, living sometimes in one barn, sometimes in another, than of town cats relocating nearby. And of course, the most pathetic are the city cats who never had a home, who were born not in love in someone's kitchen, but wherever their homeless, half-starved mother happened to be when her time came. Their life is a hard one, and I greatly admire the cat-loving people who make it their responsibility to see that a colony of homeless cats gets food at regular intervals, even though the cats never do know the security of possession and a home, or even a continuous understanding.

Some cynics say, "Oh, sure, that cat butters me up. I'm the one who feeds him." Certainly I would be less than realistic if I refused to recognize the influence of the feeding dish and who presides over it. But beyond the thank-you ankle-rub that a cat will give to anyone who feeds him, loyalty has to be earned in other ways. The cat expects to be fed. When he lives with humans, he is entirely dependent on them to provide his meals. His love and loyalty, however, must be earned by love, respect, understanding, and genuine appreciation of his willingness to live with you.

It was on this thesis that I based my attitude toward The Monster. He was obviously an unusually temperamental cat —not to say a bit off the beam. His attitude toward strangers was not normal cat attitude, but based on primitive, uncontrollably jealous loyalty. Could one ask for a more flattering fault in a cat? That loyalty of Monster's stemmed not from my feeding him, but from my sincere effort to understand him, to work with him, to show him that although we both knew he had a problem about unknown people, I did not hold it against him. I was vastly repaid during our life together for my firm belief that if a cat is given genuine love and respect, he will return it with his own love and respect. The day he died I was glad that I was with him, for he knew I was there, loving him to his last breath.

There was one cat I knew who was so loyal to the man she loved that she seldom bothered to greet anyone else. Her name was Queenie, and she was seventeen, I believe, when she died. Queenie was a magnificent pure-white angora, with blue, blue eyes. Although she lived on a farm where there are usually at least twenty other cats in the barn, she was a house cat.

Her man had a lap board on which she sat each morning to have her coat combed and brushed. She sat at table on a stool and joined the family for meals when invited. She was given the best of everything, naturally including excellent hospital care on several occasions, but the third tumor proved to be malignant. All of these attentions she took in stride as her due, but she knew that only *her people* deserved her loyalty. She would give me a cool stare of recognition on my infrequent visits to her home, but never once did she sit on my lap or make a gesture of pleasure at my presence or efforts to draw her into conversation. She was a one-man cat.

There are countless stories of personality-kid cats. Every individual cat has a distinct personality. The human error most common in people who do not understand cats is lumping them all together, saying, "cats are this, cats are that" —which simply isn't true, except in the broadest of senses.

Because of their individuality, cats are endlessly interesting when one takes the trouble to study them and is humble and open-minded enough to let them teach. Really understanding cats can open up for anyone, as it did for me, a whole new world of understanding the humans with whom we live. I believe cats are as close to humans as four-footed beings can be to bipeds, and I suspect they are way beyond us in what we call "good human relationships."

4

The Communications Systems

Since love is necessarily based on understanding, I decided a few years ago to put myself in puss' boots and see if I could gain, for a moment or longer, a cat's-eye view of humans and the world we share. It had been a long time since I had really tried to communicate with a cat, because I had thought Monster was the only cat who could talk with me, and he had died several years before. I had had kittens since, but kittens are too preoccupied with themselves, with growing up and playing and wanting things done for them, to listen to people thoughtfully. And old everlasting Minnie, sweet, adoring, beautiful, is not too bright—or so I thought. Now Jo-Jo and SuziTu were grown up, and I wondered if perchance I could engage them in serious conversation.

I have put up with a great deal of raillery from friends who are not so thoroughly possessed by cats. I do not let it bother me, because these unfortunate people simply do not know what they are missing—and never will, until a cat decides to give them an education. But on one score I am adamant: *Of course* I talk to my cats!

I talk aloud to cats in English and in cat language, as much as I have been able to learn of it. And we talk perhaps most fluently without words, in an exchange of thought that is most gratifying because, once established, the extent of communication is unlimited.

It took the chance reading of a book called "Kinship with All Life" by J. Allen Boone, to make me aware that other people have experienced the same silent-talk satisfaction that has meant so much to me, not only with cats but with many other animals I have met.

Cats seldom vocalize when they are having a heart-to-heart talk with humans or with each other, although they do speak up when they are asking for something. Most of their response is with their eyes, body attitudes, and a purely psychic thought transference, for which one must have a completely open mind, ready to accept.

Although Minnie gives me vast quantities of sympathetic understanding and is always ready to listen to me with a gentle paw on my cheek or in my hand, I am never able to communicate on the receiving end quite so freely with any female cats as I can with males. This is no reflection on female cats. SuziTu and I were in very close communion when she had her kittens and still are whenever she is in heat. Here, we share the mutual interests of femininity and motherhood, and she is primarily interested in being a female and a mother. Aside from purely feminine interests, SuziTu simply leaves to Jo-Jo the trying business of attempting to keep me in line and educate me.

Strange cats often approach me, sometimes to give me an

ankle-rub of recognition, sometimes to complain about the humans who are mistreating or misunderstanding them. It is very flattering and a bit embarrassing, because I have not yet had the courage to storm into a local shop, wag my finger under the grocer's nose, and shout, "Your cat says you're not feeding him well enough when you close the shop on weekends!" After all, I might want to shop there. This cowardice of mine may disappoint the complaining cat, but I do express sympathy, even though I know it is no substitute for a square meal on Sunday.

Usually if I stop to talk with a cat on the street, inside of two minutes there is a crowd of cat-loving people around me, exchanging anecdotes, exhibiting cat snapshots, swapping old wives' tales and sound advice about cats. They glow as they describe "the biggest cat you ever saw!" and "the tiniest kitten"—with no need for fisherman-type exaggerations about "the one that got away." We share each other's sadness when the story ends with "but he died"; and we share each other's happiness when it ends with "even at that age, she's perfectly healthy, lively as a kitten. . . ."

Sometime during this convocation the unknown cat of my interview has stretched, yawned, got up gracefully, and disappeared. No one has noticed his departure. We bored him.

My first serious-minded encounter with the silent communications system was the night when I established, once and for all, that I, not The Monster, was in command. Monnie was perhaps three months old, full of kittenish freshness. He came dancing at me from behind my chair, his back arched, his tiny teeth bared, pretending to attack as he issued a most unalarming baby-size hiss. I leaned over the arm of the chair, looked him in the eye, and hissed back.

His reaction was startling. We both knew we were playing, but he stopped in his tracks, all the pseudo-fight gone from him, and stared at me for a long time. I stared right back, not speaking. Finally I smiled and held out my hand. He jumped onto my lap and nuzzled me, and shortly we were playing boisterously again. For a few minutes we had communicated without words about a very primary matter: Who's boss around here?

Monnie always apologized for any transgression when he knew he had been wrong; and he expected me to do likewise, although he was exceedingly patient with me when I chastized him mistakenly. There was the time when I had strung our Christmas cards on ribbons and Scotch-taped them to the plaster walls, only to find them on the floor when I got home at night. I gave Monster a thorough lecture on leaving those strings of cards where I had put them. I told him sternly that it was very wrong of him to take them down, that they were Anne's and my toys, not his.

I was in the midst of further elaboration on my theme, Monster sitting calmly before me with a look of superior understanding and pity on his face, when another string loosened itself from the wall and fell to the floor. Scotch tape does not hold up well when the room is warm. It was my turn to apologize, which I did most sincerely, and was most graciously forgiven with a gentle ankle-rub.

The scope of a cat's vocabulary depends on two things: his intelligence and willingness to comprehend and to learn words, and his human's patience and insistence on teaching. Monster's vocabulary, as I have said, was superior, but he was an exceptionally intelligent cat. Minnie, on the other hand, with a slower mind but a longer life, has learned a great many words, too. Interestingly, her willingness to learn words and to respond to them did not develop until her dependence on The Monster could no longer be satisfied and she had to rely entirely on herself and me—another indication of her release from subjugation.

The surest way to any cat's heart seems to be to say "pretty kitty" in a soft, high voice. I have tried it on strange cats and almost wished I had not, because what I need least is extra felines in my cat family.

Jo-Jo is very fond of kibbled cat food, which my then six-year-old grandson said is "too fishy for me." So although I occasionally introduce a new brand of kibbled food, I still call it "Cat Chow." From anywhere in the house, Jo-Jo will come running if I say "Jo-Jo, Cat Chow?" Arriving underfoot, he speaks gently but urgently in favor of it, looking up with his eager, intense gaze and following with his eyes the journey of chow from cupboard to dish. And the current game is to get him to indicate vocally which he prefers—Cat Chow or the newest experimental introduction. I have not been able to distinguish the exact quality of difference in his preference, but there is a difference, so if it is not genuine Cat Chow, I tell him what it is and watch his reaction. He prefers the Chow, but perhaps he would like a little of the other kind, too, thank you, so I give him both.

Although I always announce that I am about to open a can of cat food, SuziTu, hearing me crank the can opener at any time, never fails to come galloping up to the counter to ask if it is cat food that I am opening. (Once she got her tail caught in the can opener, and I had to crank in reverse to free her.) So when it is not cat food, I feel it is only fair to tell her, "No, Suzi, this is grape juice" or whatever. She looks disappointed, but almost always checks up by sniffing deeply at the opened can, just to be sure I am telling her the truth.

Perhaps the most real fun in talking to cats is to learn to imitate *their* sounds. It delights them, and they take over the role of teachers with enthusiasm. Anyone who is in the least tone-deaf would probably have difficulty with this game, but if you have a musical bent or have studied languages successfully, it is duck soup. Cat language consists largely of diphthongs, with almost never a long vowel sound, and some but not all of our familiar consonants.

During the years when I weekended in the country in Mowser's people's house, Mowser was as frequent a visitor to my quarters as were his people. Often, as we all sat on the flagstoned terrace above my sloping garden, Mowser would come strolling around a corner of the house, saying, "Ma-ow? Ma-ow?" As long as I replied in a reasonably good imitation, he kept the conversation going, and his man was always intrigued by it.

"What's he saying?" he would ask.

"He says he's enjoying the smell of the garden and the feel of the sunshine, and we seem to be enjoying it, too, so he thought he'd come along and pass the time of day with us."

Mowser, having been correctly interpreted, would then settle down in a patch of sunlight, quietly listening to our conversation for a while, before he continued his patrol of the premises.

Once, Mowser's man complained about Mowser's tone of voice. "He sounds peevish," he said, very accurately imitating Mowser in a plaintive mood.

"He'll imitate your tone, if you want him to sound happier," I replied. And the following weekend, my friend reported delightedly, "You're absolutely right! He does imitate me. Listen!" The two of them then carried on a pleasant-voiced conversation in cat language, enjoying it thoroughly.

Mowser and I were extremely good friends and enjoyed many a silent conversation, too. One night when I had been sleeping soundly, I wakened suddenly and completely in the moonlit silence. There was no sound, nor had there been. I peered over the edge of the bed, not knowing why, and there was Mowser, his black coat hardly visible in the darkness of the room, his gold eyes boring into mine. Without a sound, he stood up and headed for the door, looking back over his shoulder. I stumbled out of bed after him, groping my way through the familiar rooms, just able to see Mowser ahead of me. Purposefully, he took me to one of the outside doors, sat before it, and looked up at me. "Ah-oo!" he said. I fumbled with the knob, which resisted me. Impatiently, Mowser got up and headed for another door, waited for me to open it, and went out.

In the bright moonlight (the moon was full that night), he stretched out on the grass and rolled over and over, turning this way and that in obvious ecstasy. He stretched his forelegs forward and his hind legs backward and made a long back. He turned over and scratched the back of his head on the grass. He writhed from side to side. More than a bit disgruntled because I had thought he had more serious urgencies on his mind, I returned to my slumbers. I suppose I should have been flattered that he came to me with a request he undoubtedly knew his own family would not have taken so kindly. On the other hand, I knew I had been victimized by an expert con man, and much as I love cats, I do not like to be outsmarted.

If a cat ever says "meow," it is sheer coincidence; I have often seen cats look puzzled at humans who say "meow" to them. After all, there is a long E vowel in it. But there is a wide range of sounds that seem to be universally included in cat language, and in my limited way, I have become fairly good at Siamese-cat language, which strikes a responsive chord in other cats I have tried it on.

Jo-Jo's favorite vowel (actually diphthong) sound is "aah"; SuziTu's is "ow"; Minnie's favorite comment is "Hm-m-m?"; and SuziTu's son, Mr. X, his man reports, still bleats like a little lamb as he did when he was a kitten. These individually characteristic phrases apparently can be used to mean many things as conversation openers, the differentiation being in tone of voice. The consonants with which they can be combined seem to have little meaning. A quiet utterance can be a friendly greeting or a remark that someone ought to start a conversation. Spoken with high-pitched urgency, the same sounds mean, "I'm entitled to service and here you are, starving me!" or, "Please pick me up and love me for a minute right now!"

The Siamese especially love to talk. They endlessly repeat the same phrase as long as their human responds with a good imitation. Suzanne, and later, SuziTu, learned to greet me as I entered the door with a realistic approximation of "hello." So SuziTu and I "ow-wow" back and forth until I grow weary of it and say something else.

Once when she was in heat, I lost patience with her constant "come-and-get-me" yelling. In irritation, I found myself yelling back at her in exact imitation. This turned out to be just what the little witch wanted, and it delighted her beyond measure.

"Yow!" she shouted, standing at the head of the stairs above me.

"Yow!" I replied, a little louder from my chair.

"Yow! Yow! Yaa-ooo!" she caroled, trying to out-volume me and doing very well.

Glad I no longer had close neighbors, I encouraged SuziTu, varying the noisy monotony of our screeching session by yowing in series—sometimes one yow, sometimes three, and so on. Each time, she replied not only with a similar inflection and emphasis, but with the exact rhythm too.

Joining in the cacaphony, a visiting friend called up to her, "How *now*, brown cow?" To which SuziTu replied immediately with carefully deliberate spacing, "How *now* br-r-r-ow wow?" We then began work on "The rain in Spain," but SuziTu either could not or would not change her tune, so she shut up entirely. The crashing silence that resulted was wonderfully welcome while it lasted.

I have found that normally all the cats I speak to prefer a high pitch in the voice, which seems logical since they can hear supersonic whistles, the tiny whiz of a fly's wings, or the high, inaudible whine of a button being whirled rapidly in a circle at the end of a string.

A German scientist, it was reported a while ago in *The New York Times*, has devoted years to the study of how cats communicate among themselves; and anyone who has spent any time at all watching these delightful creatures cannot fail to have observed that soundless communication exists between them.

There were times when Monnie and Minnie, happy as they were together, very obviously were not speaking to each other. Like strangers, they would cross each other's paths, noses in air, looking as though neither could see another cat in the whole kingdom. Sometimes these not-speaking spells would last for several days, and then as though nothing had happened, they would play happily together again. This was another evidence of their ability to communicate without sound, for there was never an audible cross word or a raised paw between them. It took Jo-Jo (and old age for Minnie) to bring out Minnie's full capabilities of vocalized contentiousness and invective.

Between themselves, cats also have a wide variety of sounds. Just listen for a few weeks to the commands, praises, and reassurances a mother cat gives to her kittens! The talk that goes on between adult cats is usually inaudible, except when they want to let humans in on it. I have seen Minnie and Jo-Jo sit and stare at each other for ten minutes without moving, and suddenly one gets up and stalks away or uncurls a paw and deals out a swift swat across the other's nose.

I have also seen Jo-Jo and SuziTu making love with their eyes—not touching, just smiling at each other unblinkingly, minutes on end—and then one goes to the other and nuzzles, or they touch noses, or begin to wash each other.

Cats smile with their eyes, although when they laugh aloud, they open their mouths. There are many different kinds of eye-smiling. Sometimes their eyelids slowly come together to cover the eyes. Sometimes the lower lid alone arcs upward, and the pupils become mere vertical slits. And sometimes the eyes, wide open, simply sparkle with mirth or love.

As most people know, a cat's eye pupil contracts or expands according to how much and how bright a light is reaching it. But it is my own observation that the light from within the cat's mind and emotional state of the moment has much the same effect. When a cat is angry, frightened, or otherwise upset, very little of the iris shows around the enlarged black pupil. But when he is relaxed and happy, the pupil is likely to contract, often becoming vertical instead of round. And when he smiles, his eyelids take on a more elliptical shape than the serious round-eyed look of sobriety or deep consideration.

Sometimes a cat finds a more overt way of making his wishes known to humans. I remember the day when Monster frantically paced from the living room to the apartment door and back again, over and over, until I finally got the idea that something was wrong. "What is it, Monnie?" I asked.

He answered with an urgent little cry and headed for the door again, making sure I was following. I opened it. Minnie sat, patient and speechless, in the outer hall. She had ducked out when I went to the incinerator, and I had not noticed that she was not with me when I returned. She had not made a sound out there in the hall—at least, none for my ears. But Monnie knew, and he knew how to get my help in a job that he could not do for her himself.

There was also the affair with his former girl friend, Aleen. Aleen was a coy, frightened-looking little girl cat who shyly flirted without being introduced, and we named her for one of Anne's schoolmates. She appeared on an adjoining rooftop that happened to be level with our living room window, just across the narrow courtyard, not too long before Minnie came to claim Monster's full attention and affection.

Monster eyed Aleen longingly through the window, which I kept carefully closed. I never heard a sound out of either of them, but suddenly Monnie would leap for the window-sill perch, and there would be Aleen on the opposite roof, flipping her femininity at him. I wonder if he told her that he had been altered? Or did he know?

Is it entirely a matter of sensitively tuned hearing or is some degree of communication involved when a cat jumps down and runs to the door of the apartment a full minute before his loved human emerges from the elevator in the outer hall? I think it is silent communication. When people enter a building, heading for home, certainly their thoughts turn, even if unconsciously, toward the home front. With the two elevators in my last apartment building constantly running up and down their shafts, carrying people to and from more than a hundred apartments, how else could my cats know that I was on any particular elevator trip before the cage had risen seven flights to my floor and its automatic door had slid open?

Conversely, my cats know when I am planning a more-than-routine trip away from home, even before I start making bag-packing motions. They pace the floor, follow at my heels, look worried, and talk a blue streak at me in scolding or sadly complaining tones. So I have always made it a point when I leave the house even for a few minutes to say good-by to them and to add, "I'll be back." It means the difference between security and insecurity to them, once they have learned it. And it does not take long for them to understand the meaning, even though there is not always a close association with my return. Perhaps I have helped them to understand it more quickly by saying, as soon as I have shut the door behind me on entering, "Hi, everybody. I came back." Or "Hello, Jo-Jo; ow-wow, Suzi. Hiya, Minnie. Madam's home."

Even when thirst arouses me in the middle of the night, I have to explain to Minnie, in answer to her "Hm-m-m?" that I am going for a drink, and "I'll be back."

Although I know from experience that cats prefer soft sound and high notes to loud and blatant noises, I know one cat who responds with dignified equanimity to the most abusive terms shouted at him in a loud, harsh voice. It does not disturb him in the least because he knows the man with the bellow really has a heart of gold and would probably grab his shotgun and bang away at the first person to lay a finger on the cat he loves so noisily.

On the other hand, poor Jo-Jo was startled out of his gentlemanly complacency once by a teen-age guest who roared commands at him as soon as they had been introduced. The girl was accustomed to large-scale dogs, and when Jo-Jo ran under a chair, frightened by her shouting, she said proudly, "See? You have to let them know who's boss!"

5

SuziTu's Kittens

The night before I went to a late-July convention in Cincinnati, SuziTu sat down before me as though to receive final instructions. She braced her forepaws a bit apart to steady herself, compensating for the pear-shaped bulge in her normally almost emaciated body. She looked up at me, slanted blue eyes, wide and questioning, now ruby in the lamplight.

"SuziTu," I said firmly, "either you have those kittens tonight or you wait until next Wednesday when I'll be home again!"

"Waa-ow!" said SuziTu earnestly, looking alarmed.

I wondered whether she was kidding me, for I was the jittery one.

Her pregnancy had not worried either of us, since she was obviously in excellent health and spirits. As she progressed through the waiting time, she gradually began to eat more heartily and to drink more milk and water. She looked scarcely any plumper, but felt a bit heftier when I picked her up.

Although she remained playful and affectionate with both Jo-Jo and me, she tamed down her high jumps after a time and became a trifle more sedate than usual. Otherwise, she was unchanged by the impending big event, and only the pinkness of her nipples, now a little more prominent than usual, suggested approaching motherhood.

As the days ticked off, however, I noticed that she sat with her feet apart, not the usual Siamese sitting posture. The night before the convention, which opened on a Sunday, her bulge was most pronounced at the rear. All was according to "the book," but I still had no answer to my major question: Would I be home when the kittens came?

It was the first litter for both of us, and I had read everything I could find on the subject and listened to too many old wives' tales. "When she shows a convincing bulge," the book said, "expect the kittens in four or five weeks. . . . When her teats begin to swell, kittens are not far off."

What is a "convincing bulge" in a whisper-thin Siamese? How far off is "not far off"?

"The first litter may be a little early or a little late," the book said reassuringly, informing me that gestation normally takes sixty-three days. But when, during the long and touchingly tender courtship, had Jo-Jo actually started this litter cooking? How could I count the days if I did not know when to begin?

And then there were the horrifying suggestions of well-meaning friends. "You know, sometimes the father eats the kittens, because he's jealous." And "How is your old cat Minnie going to like kittens?" Minnie had of late become quite irascible. She had been queen of the roost ever since Monster died. So I worried. I wanted to be on hand when those kittens were born, partly to see the miracle of birth and partly to make certain that the rest of the cat family reacted properly. I went to bed feeling dejected, not looking forward to the convention at all.

I had made a nice, soft pad of washable clean rags and topped it with an old bedspread that would smell homey to SuziTu, who had slept on it every night of her life with me. On top of the nest, I had also spread a soft cotton-flannel sheet, carefully arranging the whole affair, as the book instructed, so that kittens could not pull it over themselves and smother.

I had watched SuziTu's pregnancy-motivated explorations and decided she simply could not mean to have her babies in what I called the "hot closet," which was next to the incinerator wall and must have got well above 90 degrees when the incinerator was operating, which was twice a day.

So I decided the best delivery room was my bedroom closet. The book said it had to be dark, quiet, secluded, and surrounded by comforting walls. I put the nest in a three-foot-square corner, and barricaded the fourth side by pulling up the edges of the nest. Did I know whether newborn kittens could roll over the edges of their bed? I took no chances. This bed had the advantage of being accessible to mine, and I was eager to have the nursery close, in case SuziTu needed me in the night. I showed the bed to her, and she was interested, but noncommital.

My clock radio nudges me each morning at 6:25 with soft music. Until that time, nothing—absolutely nothing—can wake me. But the music I heard on convention morning was unusual, and twenty minutes early. It was a strange, unearthly, somewhat Oriental sound, and it came from under the bookcase headboard, rather than from the radio. I bounded out, wide awake.

"Suzi! Come out quickly! Suzi!" Her sides were heaving convulsively, and I could not reach her. Obediently, she squeezed herself under the headboard framework. I snatched her up and galloped around the bed to the closet, where her nest waited. There were three of us when I set her down with the first of her tiny bundles. She stretched out on her side and began to lick the new baby.

With an apprehensive glance at the clock, I dialed my daughter's phone number. "I'm taking you at your word," I told her when she responded sleepily. "Suzi's having her kittens *now*, and you said you wanted Kurt to see them born." Fifteen minutes later, Anne and my six-year-old grandson joined me in the bedroom, set up housekeeping on the floor before the closet door, and watched SuziTu. SuziTu cried softly as each kitten appeared, not in a voice of alarm or pain, but in a gentle "wow" that was different from her usual conversational gambits.

As each emerged from under her tail, she moved a bit, still lying on her side, in order to reach the baby with her rough tongue. She licked hard, and in a moment the transparent sack disappeared, the kitten struggled to find its first food, and SuziTu severed the umbilical cord with her teeth. Then she returned to concentration on her first-born.

The third kitten took SuziTu by surprise to such an extent that she rolled over on it while I was out in the kitchen making fresh coffee, and only when the fourth appeared did we find the little cold body behind her. For the sake of Kurt's equanimity, I stifled my desire to mourn; he was full of curiosity, examining the expired kitten with me in minute detail—seeing the tiny ears folded flat back against the walnut-size skull, feeling the toothpick bones, and admiring the minutely complete paws. The tiny creature was almost translucent, and we marveled at the completeness of the little claws, the closed lids over bulging eye sockets, the head snug between outstretched forepaws, the tail tight against the side of the body, and the hind legs drawn up close under the little belly. Newborn Siamese kittens look like little white rats as they gradually unfold, but on emergence, they are egg-shaped. Until they were three weeks old, I could hold all four at once in the palm of one hand.

SuziTu never gave a sign of knowing about the one that died. As a matter of fact, it seemed as though she thought the first baby was the *only* one, for as each of the five was born, she industriously licked the first (comparably) big bruiser, making his fur rise fluffy and white around his body, while he eagerly sought and found his meal. The others, it seemed, could shift for themselves, and I watched attentively to be certain that they did, knowing that within the first half hour, every kitten must have his first drink of mother's milk or not survive.

The fifth kitten was indeed excess baggage as far as his mother was concerned. She must have read the book, too, and been assured that the first litter is usually not more than two. We knew that this was the last kitten when it was followed shortly by its placenta, which SuziTu ate and eventually regurgitated, as is normal.

The birth process for cats is a surprisingly tidy one. There was only a little colorless fluid that dampened the top covering of the nest when the last kitten had been born, so I carefully changed the top sheet for a fresh one, disturbing the family as little as possible. Aside from a few loose hairs from SuziTu's coat, which I had brushed faithfully thoroughly throughout her pregnancy, there was never a spot on that top sheet. While changing it, I tried to arrange the final kitten in position to nurse, without avail. But little last-on-the-list was not to be ignored. Peeping and nuzzling blindly, he searched out the source of sustenance. His tiny mouth seemed always to miss its goal, and he peeped frantically.

"That kitten just has to eat," I said, and romped out to heat some milk in the kitchen. Filling a medicine dropper with warm milk, I popped it into the gaping little maw and squirted. It is a wonder I did not choke the poor baby! "We'll probably lose this one, too," I said, "but at least I got some milk into him."

By eight o'clock, it was all over and time for me to pack. While I did so, I kept an eye on the nursery scene and was ready for any emergency when Daddy Jo-Jo came to visit. Timidly, he tiptoed toward the closet, sniffed his productive little mate, and kissed her gently on her nose. She purred at him. He sniffed at the nursing babies as though at any moment they might explode under his face. Then he quietly disappeared into the living room, taking my fears with him. I knew he was never going to menace those kittens.

But where was Minnie during all this excitement? I looked for her and found her blandly ignoring the whole commotion, warming her old bones on top of my light-garden cabinet. When she was sure she had my full attention—because I spoke to her affectionately and reassuringly—she waltzed out to the kitchen with me pattering at her heels. She looked over her shoulder to make certain I was still watching and jumped from the floor to the top of the refrigerator, five feet up, and without a pause took the next two feet, lifting herself to the top of the broom closet. From this vantage point, she grinned down at me with a positively lip-smacking leer that said, "Humph! Look what *this* old lady can do!" I have never before or since seen a cat jump straight up to such a height, although the top of the broom closet was a favorite place, reached via the step-stool, the sink, and the counter en route to the adjacent refrigerator top.

So I flew off to Cincinnati, full of awe at the wonders of nature and convinced that the poor little last-born kitten would not be awaiting my return. I had given Anne instructions for disposing of the starved little body when necessary, because when I left, he still had not found how to utilize his mother's counter service.

Returning on Wednesday, I found this note from Anne, who had been in charge of the family during my absence:

Dear Mom:
SuziTu is under the bedspread with her family. I tried, I really did; on Tuesday, when Kurt and I arrived to check up on progress, there she was. I immediately remembered how you had hoped she wouldn't have her kittens *there* because of the potential mess, and decided there was still the possibility of a potential mess, so I upped and tried to relocate them in the nest in the closet.

What an uproar! Suzi would have none of it. You'd think I was taking the knife to her children, skinning them for winter coats. Wow-wow-wo-oow! I only got away with picking up one little one and depositing it in the closet, but the minute I turned my back, Suzi had picked the baby up in her mouth and was running around and around your bed with it, waiting to see what I'd do next.

She started under the bed, then jumped up, kitten still

> in mouth, to put it on top of the cover; then decided that wasn't safe enough until I'd calmed down—anyway, I gave in and that's why the kittens are under the bedspread. . . .

Only they were not. Nor were they under the bed or in the nest in the closet. SuziTu was gleefully rubbing against my ankles, peering with me under the bed, under dressers, into corners, purring like a motor. "Guess where, Madam, guess where!" I hid my annoyance and anxiety. Anne's note had said nothing about whether Number Five had lived or not. I begged SuziTu to stop playing this crazy game and *show* me where they were.

SuziTu rolled over gleefully, wanting her belly scratched, purring louder than ever. "Oh, no, I won't tell. You've got to guess."

"O.K., Suzi," I said, pretending to give up the search. "I've got to unpack my bag." Which I proceeded to do, keeping the corner of an eye on this witchy little mother all the time. Recognizing that the game had worn itself out, and (as I found repeatedly, later) being a fantastically devoted mother who spent every moment with her children's welfare uppermost in her mind, SuziTu started purposefully out of the bedroom. As purposefully, I followed her to the warm, deep storage closet that I had considered too hot for her nursery.

"Oh-ho, Suzi!" I crowed. "So this is where you've hidden them!" But they were nowhere visible. She glanced at me over her shoulder, pointed her chin to the deepest, darkest corner, hesitated, and finally allowed her maternal instinct to reveal the ultimate secret. They were tucked into the deep, softly lined pocket of my sewing box.

Over their mother's worried protests, I picked the kittens

out one at a time and counted four. So the last-born *had* survived after all. I put them back into the pocket. Next day, she had moved them to the opposite corner of the closet, and thus began a series of seventeen moves from place to place. Inevitably, if I touched her babies, she felt impelled to move them to a new hiding place. I had read that she would, but I couldn't resist.

I knew that until their eyes were open—and for a week or so thereafter—they should not be exposed to bright lights. So I had rigged a little 5-watt night light to help me see them when I wanted to. It was a month before SuziTu changed their home to a more brightly lighted place.

Her moving was always clearly motivated. The constant change of home during that first experience with kittens must have annoyed her, because I created it unnecessarily, trying to hurry the babies' development. When they were a couple of weeks old, I began each evening to take them, one at a time, to the living room. I wanted to play with them. SuziTu, patently annoyed, worried, but very patient with me, came scurrying after each kidnaped one, took it in her mouth by the neck, and dragged it back home. Always the next day, the nest had been moved during the night —sometimes to a former location because she ran out of new ideas.

Not until it became obvious to her that the kittens were able to climb from the sewing box, to which she had returned them—and having climbed to the top, to fall to the hard floor fifteen inches below—did she finally allow them to reside in one of the many tempting boxes I had proffered hopefully, if belatedly. At last, when they were staggering joyfully around the living room, exploring here and there and becoming more than she could cope with in her shuttling back to the nest, she corralled them under the sofa.

Now she considered them old enough for wider territory. With soft little warning clucks, like a mother hen, she trained them to assemble there under one end, quiet as the little mice they had resembled at birth.

By now, they were almost too big for SuziTu to carry in her teeth, even though they tried to cooperate by curling up their little hind legs so that they would not drag on the floor.

Finally, SuziTu moved them for the last time to the kitchen, where they took up residence under the sink, close to the feeding station. She pulled down a collection of clean scrubbing rags for them to sleep on. For fun, there was an empty jardiniere stored under the sink that usually contained a kitten or two. Now she taught them to eat from feeding dishes, showing them first how she did it, crooning, watching to see that they imitated. The under-sink safety zone was the final formal nest. After a while, she did not care where they slept, but if one was missing, she searched restlessly until she had located it.

SuziTu took to motherhood as though she were an old hand. I never cease to marvel at her intuition and made many a note on it in my cat-production diary. There was, of course, much that I had to learn. I had read and reread the books on which I have always relied to tell me when to call the vet, how to administer first aid, and how and when to feed cats and kittens. But none of them told me just how to handle the inevitable mess that kittens would make until they were old enough to be house-trained. To be sure, I had read that "some kittens are born housebroken," but I was dubious.

The "inevitable mess," I soon discovered, was SuziTu's problem, not mine. Instinctively, SuziTu knew exactly how to handle it. There was never the slightest mess at all, although I checked diligently, day after day, until I caught onto SuziTu's technique. Her family's tidiness began right at the source whenever it was necessary. When a kitten had anything to eliminate, SuziTu diligently and patiently washed its little rear, ingesting so that she herself could do the final eliminating in the proper place. She never missed, because she was seldom away from her babies for more than a few moments during the first few weeks of their lives. I learned to recognize the special little peep of a kitten who has to go; and SuziTu always heard it first.

I had placed a litter box close to their nest in the closet, but SuziTu preferred her own in the bathroom, so I put the box away for a month until the babies were ready to be box-trained. By that time, they were living under the sofa in the living room, and SuziTu taught them to use the box I hid there for them. It helped her to box-train them earlier than if they had had to wait until they were moved to the kitchen, where I had placed another comfort station.

Once, while the kittens were living under the sofa, I watched SuziTu tuck them in and head without a backward glance for her feeding dish in the kitchen. She got halfway across the room before the first little head appeared from under the sofa skirt, a head that watched her disappear into the distance, vanished under the sofa, and reappeared with three replicas. "The old lady's gone–come on out, fellas!"

This began the endlessly amusing play periods in which their mother taught them to chase a little ball or to pounce on a wad of paper, allowed them to roam, chased and cuffed them, and summoned them with her special little commanding croon, which they obeyed instantly. The training process was another of her intuitive programs, and she gave herself to it with patience, knowingness, and authority. It was beautiful to watch.

As her confidence in their self-dependence increased, so did her pride in showing them off to visitors. When anyone came—and I invited all my cat-loving friends—she paraded them gleefully, put them through their paces, and commandeered them back to their nest like a little martinet, purring loudly all the time.

"The book" had said that Siamese kittens need to stay with their mother longer than other kittens because they are relatively slow to mature. So I waited until they were three months old before I advertised the kittens for sale. By that time, they were almost as big as SuziTu. Their little noses, tails, ears, and paws were smudged with slate gray, and although they continued to nurse, they ate from dishes like hungry little pigs and drank both milk and water by the quart. SuziTu was ready to forget them. She had done her job and done it well, and she was terribly thin from the extra work they had given her.

I sold the first two separately, and she did not seem to notice that there were fewer. As time wore on and I discovered no buyers for the remaining two, I found a good home for them together. When they were gone, without a regretful look in her eyes, SuziTu sashayed over to Jo-Jo and started teasing him for another family.

SuziTu had been such a wonderful little mother that I decided another litter would not be out of order. Accordingly, experienced as I now was, one day in the following December, I confidently posted a note to myself on the bulletin board: "Expect kittens by Valentine's Day."

As a matter of planned-parenthood record, the second litter actually did arrive on February 14th! This time, it was a lark. SuziTu confidently expected me to help her have her kittens and routed me out of a good book at 10:30 in the evening to follow her into the corner of the hot closet that she had preferred the first time. Here, I had set up a nicely lined carton, and here she had four healthy, bawling little ones, with much purring on her part and careful maneuvering on mine to see that each kitten got under her licking tongue as soon as it arrived.

She made no sound other than purring, but gave a soft, heaving sigh as each kitten arrived. Jo-Jo hovered, concerned, in the background, and I reported regularly to him. Then I left it to SuziTu's good discretion about when they would be old enough to move from the closet to the under-sofa post, thence to the under-sink position. She followed the geographical pattern exactly, with one brief diversion, but the timing was her own. This time, she never moved the kittens from their first nursery box until she was almost ready to escort them to the living room, even though I had played with them on occasion.

In this relaxed atmosphere, Jo-Jo seemed to come into his own as a father. Having taken little part in the job of training his first offspring, he now visited the kittens and SuziTu frequently in their nest. He seemed to share my pleasure when they started to open their bright little eyes on the fifth day, instead of waiting until the seventh. (Siamese kittens open their eyes earlier than the usual nine days for other cats.) He slept prodigiously during the first week, as though he had worried sleeplessly through his mate's pregnancy. (As a matter of fact, the night they were born, Jo-Jo had paced the hallway like any worried father.) Occasionally, he called to SuziTu, who promptly left her babies to come out and chat with their father for a brief while, nuzzling and being nuzzled in return.

Offered a tidbit, Jo-Jo refused to eat it until SuziTu joined him. His eyes glowed with love when he heard the faint peepings and little snuggling sounds in the nursery.

And he stood by, ready to help when the kittens, two weeks old, tried to climb out of their box. He hurried to the nursery whenever he heard a kitten squeal, checked up, and then returned to his loneliness. For by now, the feud that had been developing between him and Minnie had gone past the nonspeaking point to the stage of snarling (from her), swatting with an angry paw if he came too close, and a hurt look on Jo-Jo's unretaliating face.

At this point, Jo-Jo and I started to renew the former close relationship we had had in his kittenhood. He watched me make certain that his babies could not climb out of the box, fall off the bed, have too much direct light for the young eyes, or be cold. SuziTu still did not think it was time for the two-week-old kittens to be out of the box, but both she and Jo-Jo seemed to look to me as one of the team. They made every effort to tell me what they wanted, and I cooperated.

Through trial and error (SuziTu purred and licked the kittens if she approved of what I did, grabbed them away by the neck if she disapproved), I set up a workable communication system between us, and as a reward, SuziTu occasionally brought the little squirmers into my warm bed, tucked them under the covers with me, and went off to relax with Jo-Jo. There, the babies proceeded to dig their tiny sharp claws happily into my back. After two such sessions, the kittens crowding so close for warmth that I almost fell out of bed in my effort not to roll over on them, I laid down the law.

"Suzi," I said sternly, "this has got to stop. I don't mind baby-sitting for you, but I'm afraid I'll roll over on them. So I don't get any sleep. Now take them home, please, and let Jo-Jo baby-sit."

She did so without complaint, much to Jo-Jo's obvious

joy. When she had time to watch him, Jo-Jo put on a show for SuziTu, rolling and romping to please her; and when she was nursing the kittens in the nest, he liked to stand guard over his brood. So for a few nights I did not have to kitten-sit, although it was not long before she started pulling the same trick on me again, tucking her babies under the covers with me.

One night, in sheer desperation, I set up a cozy compound, safely barricaded and just spacious enough, on the bedroom floor in a corner next to the dresser. Jo-Jo loved this because he could park himself on the end of the dresser and watch over his family. By now they were three weeks old, toddling, and getting cute little distinctive color on ears, tails, and noses (the color of the paws last). Everybody liked the compound, and it made an easy transition to the living room, although SuziTu took them back to their closet nest for a few days first.

As they began their staggering little explorations, I confided to Jo-Jo that I was worried about one kitten who walked in circles instead of straight ahead like the others. Jo-Jo looked a little worried, too, and we had a thought session that ended in my teaching the wee one to walk a straight line. I simply started him off at one end of the wall, gently guiding him to stay close against it until he had reached the end, then back again. The kitten was not in the least alarmed; SuziTu and Jo-Jo watched with interest and permitted me to keep the circular walker out a little longer than the others so that he could have a lesson each evening, and it took only a few days to train him.

By the time the babies were a month old, they were wrestling not only among themselves, but also with their father. If they turned too quickly, they fell over, but it did not worry them a bit. At this age, they responded with gleeful peeps to their mother's call and to mine. Now Jo-Jo began to take his turn with SuziTu at mothering them. He washed them. He helped SuziTu train them to use their litter box. He played with them gently, as though afraid he might hurt them. He was as alert and worried as his mate when the cry of a lost kitten came appealingly from under some previously unexplored place.

When the kittens were a month old, I decided definitely that at least two of them were males. (As it turned out eventually, all four were males, as opposed to the first litter, which included only one.) While they are tiny, it is really impossible to tell their sex, but as they grow, it becomes easier. The males, whose testicles remain in their abdomens for the first three months, have two dots like a colon beneath the tail; the females, an upside-down exclamation point.

They played like little roughnecks, even chased Minnie once in a while—a dangerous pastime against which their parents had obviously warned them, for they seldom bothered her. Fearless and growling, tiny backs arched and legs braced, they tackled their father, who increased the boisterousness of his play in accordance with theirs and sometimes beat a hasty retreat when he saw them descending on him. Whether he was afraid he would hurt them or they would hurt him was a good question that I did not ask him to answer. After all, a cat without his dignity has lost his most precious attribute.

At least to a cat-lover, there is nothing more charming than a flock of kittens at play. By the time they were a month old, their 26 baby teeth had grown to be tiny needles. (They get their full set of 30 permanent teeth between the fifth and six months.) Their pretended ferociousness was savagery in miniature. Although kittens seldom hurt each

Anything not normally exposed is irresistibly fascinating to investigate—and if it's soft, it makes a delightful napping place

The top of the refrigerator has always been a favorite perch for my cats, even though paws and tails are endangered if I open the door

When it's good, it's very very good; and when it's bad—it's something horrid to cover up and bury quickly

Going up is easy, because a cat's claws are built for it; coming down may sometimes mean a call to the fire department ladder crew

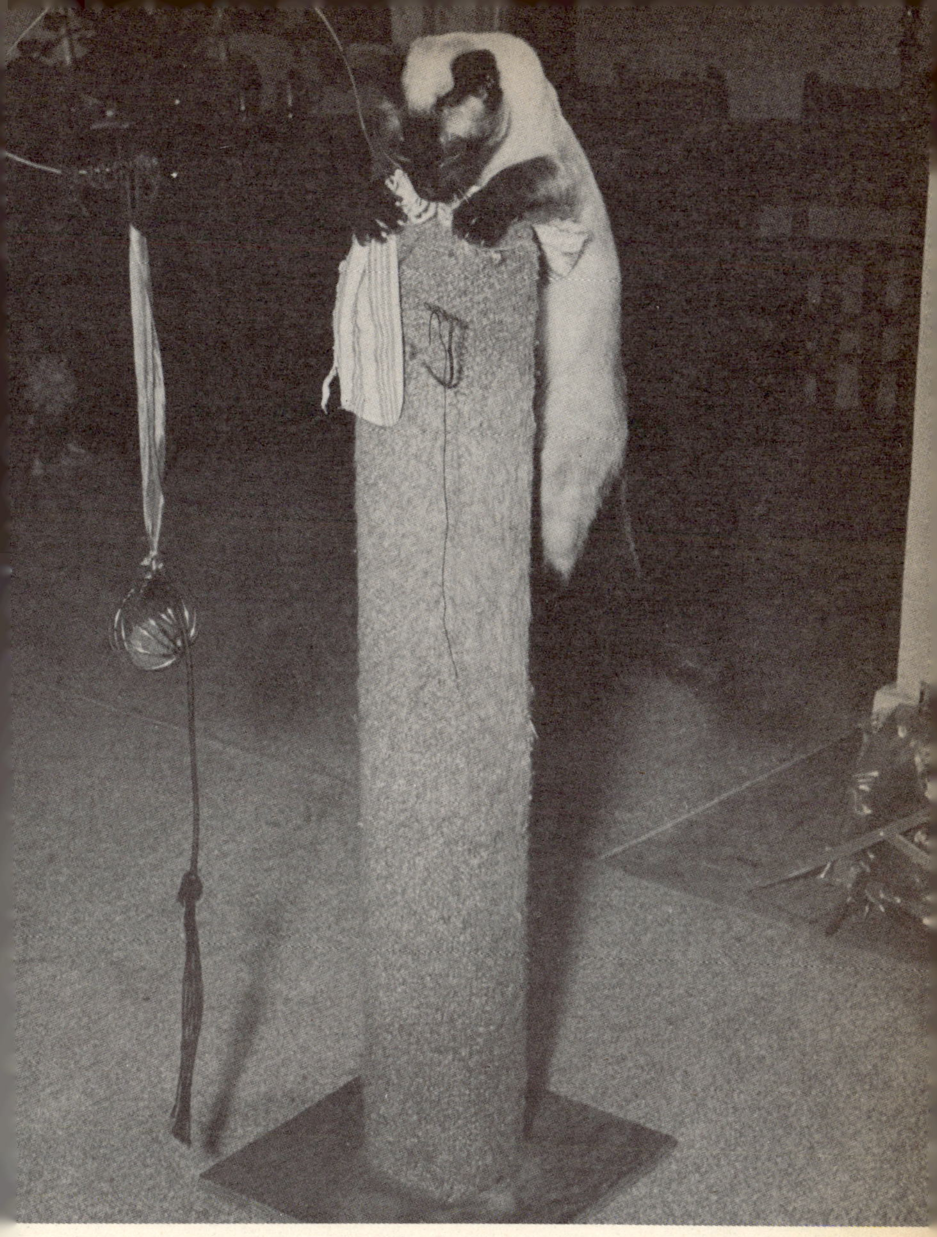

Getting a cat to use his scratching post may be difficult at first, so it helps to have something interesting and mobile on its top

If you object to having to drop everything in order to let the cat out, build a cat door that swings in both directions

My cats are polite to each other—when they all want to go into the house at once through the cat door, they line up to take their turns

It's easy for a cat to get out on a limb, but he looks to his human to extricate him when he's in difficulty

Just introduce a new-to-them object that makes a sound, and your cats have a new toy

When cats love each other, they'd rather fight than switch; they literally live for each other and often die of heartbreak if a mate is lost

When her parents are engrossed in each other, Mac takes off and leaves them to their own devices

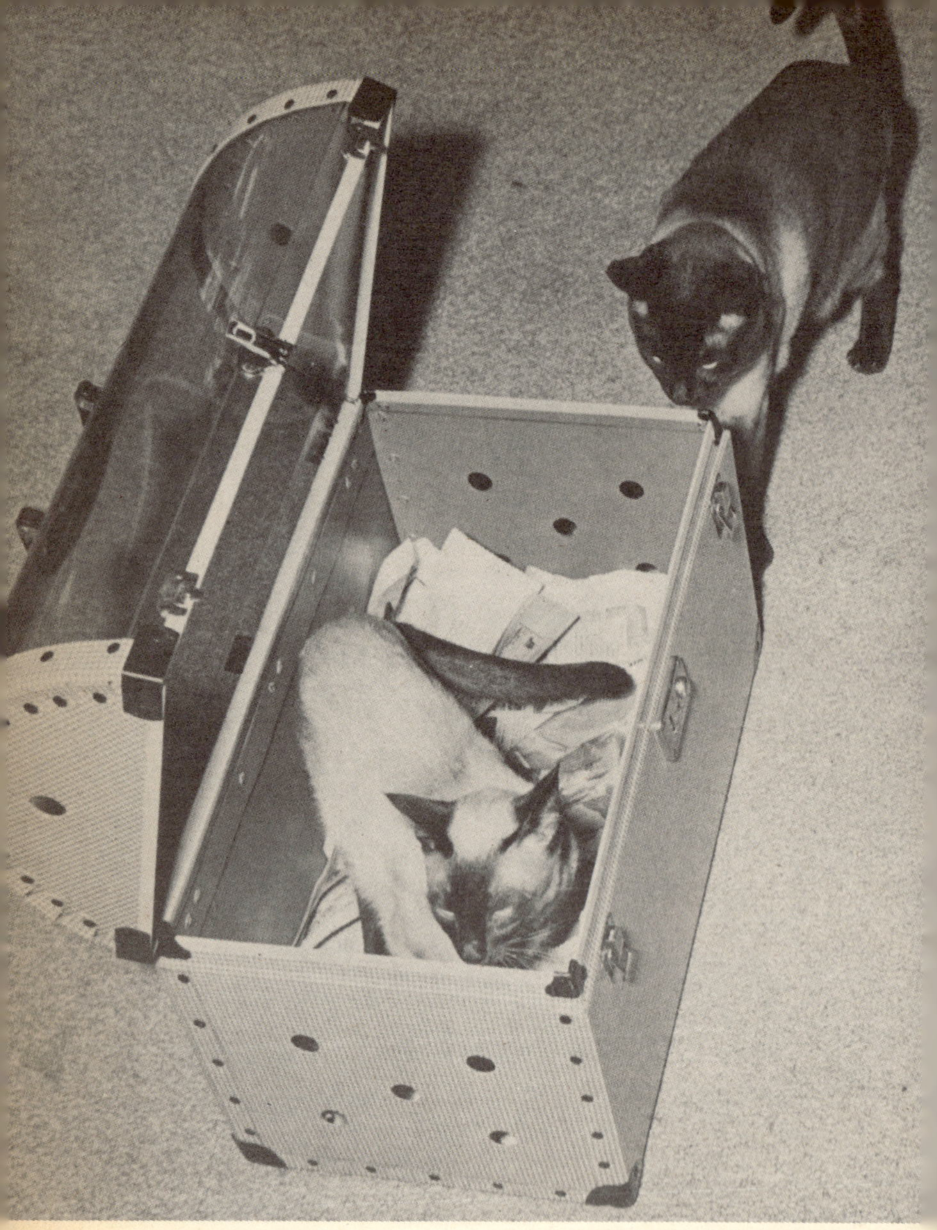

Cats don't like to leave home under human instigation, but they want very much to know all the details when another cat goes tripping

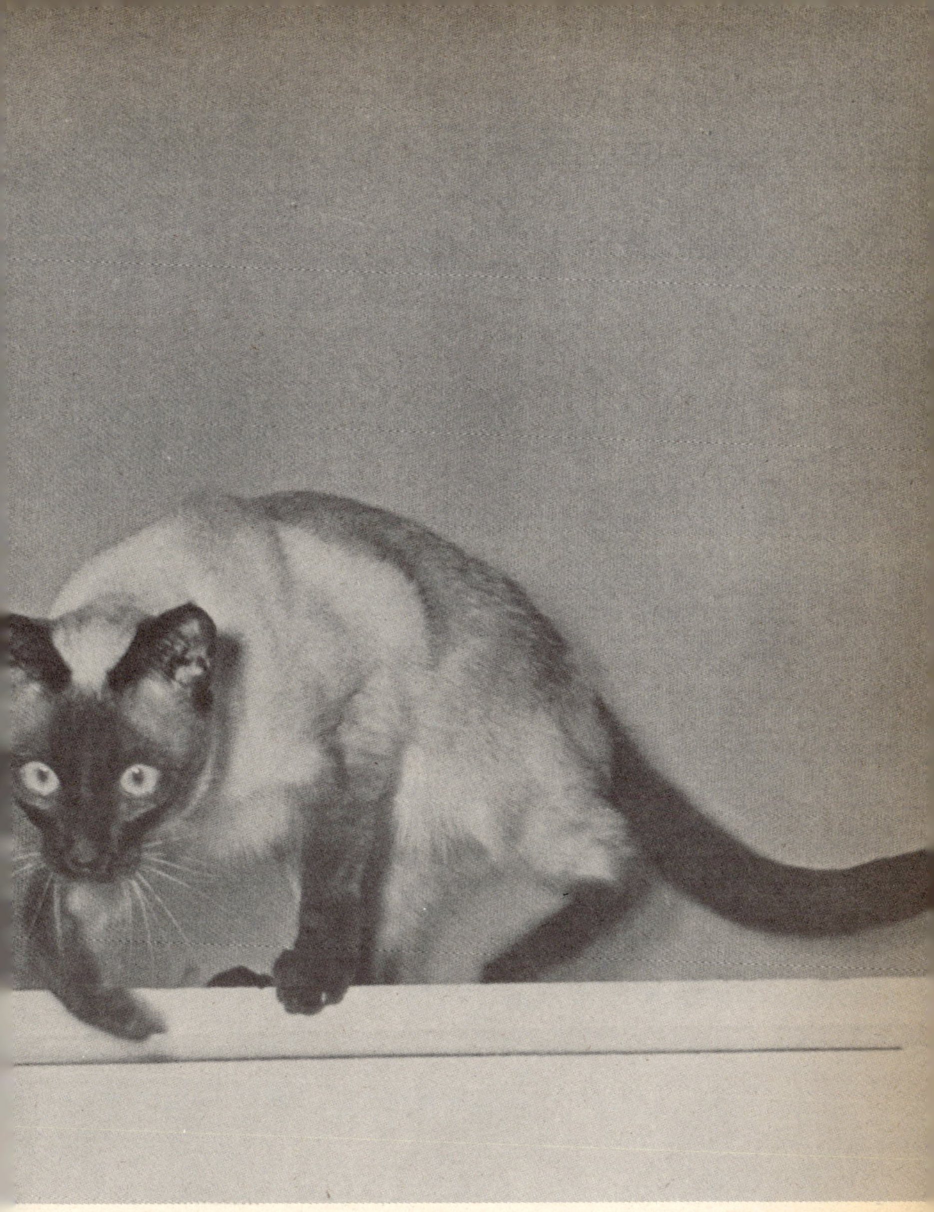

It's fun to watch the birds outside the windows—but once they've been spotted, it's time to go where the action is

Cats and dogs can tolerate each other if they become acquainted when they are young enough

Some cats open the doors for themselves and some need service, but unless they live in the city, they all enjoy going outdoors

When a mother cat has kittens to nurse, she lets nothing interrupt her own mealtime

other in play, two of ours turned up looking like little pirates one morning, each with an eye swollen almost shut by a lacerated lid. I looked at them carefully, found the eyeballs undamaged, and in a few days their mother had licked their wounds away. But twice I had to break up a too-rough game when I saw them going for each other's eyes with those sharp little teeth.

Some of their games developed accidentally, as did the one that so delighted Mr. X. Mr. X (so called because he was charmingly cross-eyed) was the last kitten to leave me and the only one in this litter that I named, because naming them made the eventual parting too difficult. (Also, Mr. X knew his name by the time he was four months old, and his purchaser was stuck with it.) Mr. X was teasing his father, standing on a small table next to the chair in which Jo-Jo was reclining. Jo-Jo flapped his tail in annoyance and accidentally struck a pewter ashtray under Mr. X's nose. It made a nice tinkling sound, and the game was on for as long as Jo-Jo was willing to keep his tail flapping.

You can almost see Siamese kittens grow. Their slate-gray coloring is just the faintest tinge when it first shows at the end of four weeks, but quite rapidly it becomes more marked and distinct. Before Mr. X left me, he had the faintest suggestion of stripes on his legs—not at all unusual, since the most careful breeding has never completely eliminated the ancestral influence of the tabby. In most solidly marked cats, it scarcely shows at all, but close examination will often reveal it, even in thoroughbreds.

Their progress with feeding, too, develops rapidly, and as their mother begins to teach them to eat from dishes, the food sometimes has to be tamed down a little until they adjust to it. The change from mother's milk to cow's milk and solid food may give them a touch of diarrhea until they become accustomed to it. Even as she was teaching them to eat, SuziTu continued to nurse them, too, during the final stages of weaning. Leaving their dishes behind, they would wind up the feast with their mother, who increasingly startled and disappointed them by suddenly getting up and walking away, leaving four little gaping mouths in surprised faces.

When they are four months old, kittens begin to become ungainly teen-agers, with long legs, outsize paws, and awkward gait. They outgrow it, or rather, grow up to normal proportions, in a few more weeks, and I find them as charming in the gawky stages as in their cuddly cream-puff babyhood when their coats are still soft baby fur and their voices high and chirping. But then, of course, I just love cats—any kind, any size, any shape or color.

It is not one of the major joys of living with a female cat to have her in heat, but fortunately it does not last long. SuziTu moans loudly for about five days, and then all is calm again for six or eight weeks. (Frequency and duration of this mate-hunting season are an individual matter. Suzanne was in heat only once every six months; and some cats, I have read, are in heat only once a year.)

There is little her human can do for her during heat except tolerate it, and the only reason for putting up with it is to have kittens. If she is an only cat in the household, and you do not want her to have kittens (which she should not be allowed to do more than twice a year at most), better keep the windows and doors closed during her season, or have her spayed. I know of a cat who jumped out of a second-story window to rendezvous with a neighbor's tom who had responded to her call.

Her noise is horrendous when she is calling, and she paces

restlessly from room to room, occasionally shouting in a hoarse voice, sometimes rolling over onto her back, sometimes dragging or elevating her hind quarters. Her whole personality changes from sweet cooperation and playful abandon to irascible, urgent demand. Nothing pleases her, and her discomfort is obvious. She slinks. She refuses to eat. She will not be cajoled. She forgets all her favorite tricks and toys, has an absolutely warped sense of humor, and takes obvious pleasure in being as noisy and self-pitying as possible. It is a trying time for anyone to whom she complains, but an extra measure of petting and affectionate words from her human–grudgingly accepted for a few moments and then angrily rejected by her–helps to ease her anguish, if she has no operative mate.

Because it was my doing that made Jo-Jo a neuter, I felt that I should try to make it up to SuziTu in whatever way possible. So I gave her extra affection, petting, and brushing during her first unrewarded season or two. In so doing, I learned that her interest in mating is not a sex-for-the-fun-of-it interest at all. She most urgently wants to have kittens. She makes this mother urge delightfully clear by rolling onto her back as she lies on the sofa beside me, purring loudly when I gently stroke her upturned belly, and working her forepaws slowly out and in toward her, exactly as she used them to pull her nursing babies closer to her while she fed them.

Once I had caught onto the comfort I could give her so easily, she developed a habit of coming to me frequently when in heat, climbing up beside me and inviting me with a most appealing smile to stroke her underside. It has taken a lot of the anguish out of her mating call.

SuziTu has now been in heat several times since Jo-Jo was altered. Wanting to be helpful, he tries the impossible still and then looks at her with sympathetic adoration. She appears not to resent that he cannot satisfy her urge, and in fact, seems to love his conciliatory attempts. They calm and pacify her for a while. I have not had her altered simply because she is *such* a good mother, and now that we live in the country, we are in position again to have her raise another delightful family of kittens, whom Jo-Jo will foster-father just as Minnie foster-mothered him.

For a male cat, the urge to mate seems to take the form of a constant willingness if he has not been altered. An outdoor tom will take himself off for a few days when he hears a calling female, even though she may be several miles away. He will return battle-scarred and dirty, when he has fought it out with all the other toms who responded to the call, and you will probably never know whether he won the lady or not. And he will do some lusty yowling of his own, usually on a moonlit night under a bedroom window.

In the confinement of an apartment if he is never allowed out, his problems sound louder than they do from the back fence outdoors. Poor Jo-Jo suffered normally while he waited for SuziTu to grow up, especially when, still not ready for motherhood, she began to flirt shamefully with him. It was at that time that he found his solution.

That was the year when all the shops were selling bedroom slippers for men, women, and children, made of some sort of synthetic lamb's wool in shockingly bright colors. They were big, puffy, soft, colorful, ridiculously like snowshoes, and very warm. I had a pair in shocking pink, but they were so warm that I could not wear them in the well-heated apartment. So when Jo-Jo adopted one of the pair as a reasonable facsimile of a soft and willing little mate, I granted him official permission, and that became his slipper.

Jo-Jo would put up with SuziTu's teasing until he could no longer take it, whereupon he would locate his slipper and growl softly at it. Straddling it with one end grasped firmly in his teeth, he waddled with it to a strategic position a few inches from SuziTu so that he could feast his eyes on her while he pretended it was she. This pacifier worked very well, except that he sometimes embarrassed me by dragging it out for use when I had guests; but it took the time-pressure off SuziTu's normal maturing.

When SuziTu finally decided she was ready and started making passes at Jo-Jo, he dutifully dragged out his slipper instead of accepting her proposal. SuziTu, angered and frustrated, screamed at him the more loudly, and went into paroxysms of fury. Jo-Jo merely renewed his frantic efforts on the slipper, looking puzzled at SuziTu's displeasure. For a while, I did not interfere, thinking he would soon catch on to the new idea. At last, fearing that SuziTu would explode and Jo-Jo would undoubtedly father a litter of whoofy pink baby booties, I confiscated the slipper and hid it. Poor Jo-Jo was lost without his pacifier, but only for a short time. Eventually, he discovered that SuziTu was every bit as much fun as the slipper, and I did not return it to him until the kittens were born. Before I finally had him altered, he had worn out the other one, too.

Jo-Jo has been especially affectionate to me since I had him altered. It was a difficult decision to make. He had fathered two litters of handsome kittens, and had I been living in something larger than a three-room apartment, I should have welcomed as many more as SuziTu cared to produce.

But the feud with Minnie had reached the stage, during SuziTu's second bout with motherhood, where there were constant cat fights—old Minnie ending up on the bottom of the heap, after goading Jo-Jo and his loyal little helpmeet to utterly frenzied distraction. Not only was the battlefield noisy enough to cause possible complaints from the neighbors if they should recognize the sounds, but I got bitten in the process of separating the combatants, and the bites became infected. "This," I said to all and sundry, "has got to stop." Having Jo-Jo altered, I reasoned, and Dr. Roth agreed, would take some of the fight out of him.

There was another equally important reason: An unaltered male cat, no matter how well-bred and handsome, when he matures, sprays. He squats on or backs up to things and squirts on everything and anything (Jo-Jo especially liked manuscripts and magazines), leaving a puddle with a very strong odor that is almost impossible to banish, even with the best of air-fresheners. In an apartment house, especially one in which the management takes a dim view of pets, the smell of cat is not to be countenanced. Altering the cat eliminates the spraying, and consequently, the odor.

So without further ceremony, the day after the most ferocious cat battle, in which I and Minnie were wounded, I carted Jo-Jo off for a few hours' visit with Dr. Roth. He went uncomplainingly and swallowed his nembutal pill without a fuss before I left him. A few hours later, I collected him and brought him home, still groggy, but otherwise unimpressed with his experience.

Castration is a very simple operation by which the testicles are rendered inoperable—not visibly removed—and it usually leaves the cat with a much sweeter disposition and no inclination to start any fights. I regretted that Jo-Jo could father no more kittens, but on the other hand, the advantages of a quiet, pleasant-smelling home had to be considered. The operation was successful as far as his spraying was concerned. He makes no male smell at all. But the feud between Jo-Jo and Minnie continued, although I was convinced it was at least half her fault.

6

Dinner Bell

I have given up putting olives into martinis. I no longer keep a little dish of raisins within nibbling reach. In fact, I stand guard over crackers and cheese and hors d'oeuvres in general, or I offer a small taste to whichever cat has a yen for the delicacy available.

Not that I am mean and selfish. I just do not think cats should eat much other than their own food, although an occasional little taste will not hurt them.

The case of the disappearing olives was a baffling one for a while. I pride myself on remembering exactly how each guest prefers his medicine and had developed a habit of arranging the glasses on the cocktail table before the guests arrived, pouring the drinks when the doorbell rang, and then opening the door. Returning, I repeatedly found the drinks where I had left them, but no olives in the glasses. I was sure I had put the olives into those glasses, but perhaps I was getting more forgetful than I realized. Although conscious of this possibility, it soon became apparent that I was not *that* forgetful—the olives were doing a vanishing act.

Then one summer day when there were no coats to hang in the guest closet, I got back to the living room in time to see Monster delicately fishing out an olive. He shook his paw daintily, not caring for martinis, thank you, and proceeded to carry the olive in his teeth to a strategic open space on the rug. There he deposited it and began to treat it as though it were a catnip ball. He batted it. He nuzzled it with his nose. He rolled over and over in ecstasy and in general behaved like a clown. Finally, he ate it.

Thereafter, I made a practice of offering him an olive in order to protect my own interests. Monnie viewed the prospect with great excitement and came running from wherever he happened to be when I called, "Monnie, want an olive?" Minnie eventually decided that if Monnie liked olives, so did she; but she was not going to be so aggressive about it. When Monnie had divided an olive into pieces, Minnie delicately nibbled at what she considered her share, but merely sat and gazed at the whole one I had given to her. I was required to cut her olive in half because she insisted she could not possibly bite into it as Monnie did. (They both preferred stuffed olives and ate the pimiento first.)

Some cats are very fond of cheese, and Minnie is one of them. Sour cream left in the bottom of the little container in which it is purchased is another tasty treat to be patiently dipped out with a delicate paw. But when it came to cookies, Monnie and Minnie were like Jack Spratt and his wife. Monnie, the white cat, would eat only chocolate cookies; black Minnie, only vanilla. They did not care for complicated cookies of any kind unless they contained raisins, for they both dearly loved them.

Although cats are carnivorous, mine have definite tastes for certain vegetables. When I was having trouble keeping my house plants in leaf because the cats nibbled at them, I consulted "the book" again and learned that cats need grass, and one should always keep a pot of it handy where they can eat it as needed. It helps them clear their digestive tracts of the fur they swallow when they clean themselves, even though they are brushed frequently.

Since I made this discovery in midwinter when grass was not easy to dig up and pot, I decided to add a little shredded lettuce to their cat food. Lettuce, I reasoned, would possibly be a good substitute and certainly would do them no harm. I never had any more difficulty with the plants and saw no evidence of woopsed-up fur balls.

Pleased with my ingenuity and its success, I decided to try other vegetables—just a small quantity mixed with the food for variety. Monnie developed a passion for diced beets, but would not touch anything with carrots in it. Both he and Minnie loved fresh or frozen peas, but turned up their noses at canned peas, which admittedly are a different taste and texture altogether. They loved French-style string beans, but did not care for whole string beans and certainly not for tomatoes, although spaghetti sauce was a great favorite on the rare occasions when I gave them a taste. One of my later cats—I've forgotten whom—had a yen for licking out the dish when I cooked squash, and another liked lima beans.

Just as sometimes happens with humans, an accidental, unpleasant association turned Monnie against his beloved beets. He was feeling poorly—I think it was the time he had been wormed—and as a treat, I gave him beef liver and beets. He lost his supper and would never eat either beets or liver after that. I am sure it was not the food that upset him, but the association remained in his mind as long as he lived.

Liver is usually popular with cats in general, but not one of mine has ever cared for it unless I cooked it. Raw liver is inclined to have a laxative effect on cats, and cooked liver works in reverse, so I cook it slightly—not overdone, but cooked through. I find that cats are as individual in their food preferences as humans are. Some of my cats have liked liver excessively and loved kidneys also; some have refused to eat when I served either one.

Two foods have been extremely popular with all my cats (aside from fish, which of course is a standard favorite): chicken and lamb. Chicken presents problems because I never allow cats to have chicken bones except for the soft neck bones. Chicken bones, like those of chops, splinter too readily. Lodged in a cat's throat or stomach, they can cause swift and agonizing death. So when I cook chicken, I have to put up with cats dancing around under my feet, screaming that I am starving them, that they have not had a decent meal in days, and what kind of heartless human have they got themselves stuck with, anyhow? This goes on until I give them their share, without bones; and as soon as the table is cleared, I take the bones out of the house, because the eager little beasts have no compunction whatever about delving into the refuse can and stealing bones from it. When I spent only weekends in the country, it was my practice, coward that I am, to cook chicken only while I was there, where I could enjoy it in peace.

Whenever I roast a leg of lamb—which is seldom now, unless I have a raft of guests to help me eat it—I faithfully promise the cats that they may have the bone. Since they know I keep my promises, they usually wait with a fair degree of patience. They have very few table scraps, because I believe wholeheartedly that they should have a simple diet intended for animals, correctly proportioned and metered out in specified quantities. When I have had a meal that appeals to them, I give them the plates to lick. All they find is a pleasant taste, and it satisfies them. Lamb bone is *very* special.

Once, after several meals, the lamb bone was finally ready for Monnie and Minnie. Minnie had been expectantly watching Anne and me throughout the meal, but Monnie was napping in the bedroom. I put the bone on a plate and set it on the floor, where Minnie fought an obvious battle with her conscience. It was a firm practice between Minnie and Monnie that *he* should invariably have the first bite of anything. Even when their dishes contained identical servings of cat food, Minnie never touched hers until Monnie had tasted his and given her the go-ahead. I was never certain of the reason for this procedure. Could be Monnie was making sure the food was safe for his beloved; could be he was asserting himself as head of the household.

At any rate, Monnie must have been really sound asleep when I put that lamb bone down, and Minnie simply could not resist. She glanced nervously over her shoulder toward the bedroom, sniffed hungrily at the bone, glanced back again. Still no sign of Monnie. At last, she made her decision and feasted. She did not by any means eat all the tasty scraps of meat. There was plenty left for Monnie when she sat down to wash her guilty face. Yet when Monnie awoke and gleefully ran to the bone, he sniffed it in utter disbelief. Minnie had eaten hers first! This was an unprecedented outrage, and he would not touch that bone, even if I increased his allowance. Furthermore, he must punish the human responsible for this atrocity, and since Madam would never do such a thing, it had to be Anne.

He sat and glared at Anne throughout the rest of the meal, despite the fact that I said, "Monnie, *I* gave Minnie the bone.

Anne had nothing to do with it." He simply did not believe me. Poor guilty Minnie took herself into hiding for a while until his rage blew over, and eventually I threw out the bone of contention. Monnie would have none of it, and Minnie had had it.

I have always brought my cats up to eat anything I offered them, mostly canned dog food. But they will not eat anything that is stale, nor would I offer them foods that I know are not healthful for cats. I never give them corn, potatoes, smoked or salt-preserved meats, fat, or bread. Corn is indigestible, perhaps because they just cannot chew it up properly, and starches have no place in the diet of a house cat. Fats and fried foods are also indigestible, and although I do not know exactly why smoked or salted meats are not allowed, they are on the banned list of all cat dieticians.

There are large and sometimes violent controversies over how much and when to feed cats. Dr. Roth told me years ago, "An adult cat should have eight ounces of food every day. No more, no less." This makes sense, since the capacity of the adult cat's stomach is said to be one-half pint, only four ounces, and most cats do not eat everything at once. So eight ounces is what mine are offered, all at one time, once a day. If they do not finish a meal in twenty-four hours, it's either because they do not care for it particularly—and I try to remember which brand and flavor it was so as not to offer it too frequently—or they simply are not hungry that day. A cat will never deliberately starve, nor will he usually overeat. But each cat has very definite preferences, and if he really dislikes a food that is offered, he will often either make scratching motions on the floor or actually find some paper to tear up and use as covering for the detested food.

I know some cats who are gluttons; I know some who eat

everything in the dish within a few minutes of being served. None of my cats has ever behaved in either fashion, and I think it is because they have all lived with me since kittenhood and learned my feeding habits at an early age.

Dr. Roth disapproves of canned food of any kind and says that fresh-cooked meat and fish are more healthful. He blamed canned foods for the cases of cystitis that have occurred in my circle of cat family and friends. Although I would never set my own opinion above that of a professional man, I do not find it possible to feed my cats fresh-cooked food every day. So I compromise. Many of the canned pet foods contain ground bone, which at least one good book says is not good for a cat; and canned cat foods, more than dog foods, sometimes are disproportionately heavy on cereals and other nonmeat fillers. So I read the labels carefully and feed my cats as a general rule on various types of canned dog food. In addition, they always have a plate of kibbled food beside their dishes. Kibbled foods are a relatively complete, balanced meal and compensate well for something the cats do not like. Too, gnawing on finely kibbled dry food cleans the tartar from their teeth, stimulates their gums, and helps prevent dental difficulties.

Kibbled foods especially for cats are fairly recent arrivals at the supermarket, although kibbled dog food has been popular for a long time. The special-for-cats foods are designed to appeal to a cat's palate, either moistened with milk or water or offered dry. Jo-Jo prefers his dry and crunchy, but I cat-sat for a mother cat and her kittens whose diet was kibbled food slightly moistened with milk, to which an egg is added once a day. And my daughter's two cats do not care for milk for drinking purposes, so she pours about half a bowl of milk and fills the bowl with kibbled food. When they have eaten down through the dry portion, they continue with the milk-soaked layer and get their Vitamin D.

Until kittens have grown their permanent teeth, they seldom attempt to eat kibbled food unless it is wet down to a consistency that their baby teeth can manage.

So far, no negative reports have reached me on the quality and nourishment of these "whole-meal" foods, and they are a lifesaver if you are going away for a long weekend, since they do not spoil or get crusty on top, as fresh and canned foods do.

A dish of fresh water and a small dish of milk complete the offerings at my feeding station. Some cats are fond of milk, and some are not. It is inclined to have a laxative effect, especially if you use evaporated milk, which should be diluted with an equal amount of water.

SuziTu drinks milk only when she is nursing kittens or during pregnancy. Jo-Jo does not seem to care for more than a tongue-coating of milk each day; Minnie drinks milk at the rate of a cup or more a day, seldom touching the water dish. Milk is not a substitute for water, and I see to it that there is always an ample supply of fresh water, not too cold, beside their feeding dishes.

The question of fresh water supplies is a puzzler. Jo-Jo drinks a lot of water, always from the water dish in the feeding station. SuziTu finishes her meal and runs into the bathroom to lick the faucet in the sink, making it drip onto her little tongue. And when I have showered, SuziTu can hardly wait for me to turn off the spray before she jumps into the tub to lap up water around the drain.

Suzanne, on the other hand, with a dish of fresh water always available, invariably took her drinks from the john, precariously bracing her forepaws so that she would not fall in. There was no need for this dangerous pursuit, but I could never persuade her to drink like a lady from the water dish.

Although I know that an all-fish diet would keep the Siamese coats a lighter color, too much fish has a tendency to cause cystitis and kidney stones eventually, so I give fish to my cats only once a week. I cook a package of frozen whiting, the cheapest fish I can find that is boneless, although any filet is equally good. I poach it in a little lightly salted water for about twenty minutes. The smell of the cooking (and later, cooling) fish brings forth anguished yowls of impatience. In order to have this tasty treat ready for the morning meal, I usually cook it the night before, let it cool, and satisfy their yearnings with a preview—a teaspoonful for each cat as soon as it is cool enough to eat. This little sample is sufficient to satisfy them until the next morning, when they eagerly await the major serving. Knowing it is on the menu, they clamor at the bedroom door earlier and more loudly than usual.

It has always been my practice to feed the cats once a day, setting up the fresh servings in the morning while the coffee perks. Some people feed their cats twice a day, and the book says that kittens need six daily meals. For many years, when business took me out of the apartment in the morning, I could not predict how late in the evening I might return; and rather than keep the cats waiting for an evening meal indefinitely, I gave it to them all at once at breakfast time. They eat sparingly whenever they want to, during the day and night. If, in the evening, the food in their dishes has become a bit dry on the surface, I stir it up, but it is seldom necessary.

If their dishes are not empty when I start my morning kitchen duties, I throw away the remaining food. Each morning, the dishes must be washed clean with hot water and detergent and filled with a fresh meal at room temperature. If the food has been refrigerated, I heat it slightly, because an icy meal is hard on a cat's stomach and may come back in a hurry. I never give them the same food more than twice in succession, for they like variety.

An egg, raw or lightly cooked but never fried, offered once or twice a week, will keep their coats shiny, but my present cats care little for eggs. Cod-liver (or halibut-liver) oil is also a good diet additive, because it aids in keeping hairballs from forming in the digestive tract. Most cats love it and will eat it from a dish or lap it from a spoon.

Strained baby foods are excellent for very young, very old, and very finicky cats. Fortunately, mine are neither that old (even Minnie still has all her teeth and a hearty appetite) nor that fussy.

When I leave for a weekend, I double the quantity of food in their dishes, knowing they will eat it only when they need it. (This is one of the differences between cats and dogs, who gobble up their meals immediately and cannot be left with two days' food.) I leave them extra dishes of water and extra kibbled food and have never found them to be unhappy over being left alone–from the point of view of their meals. In summer, I leave the air-conditioning turned on so that the food will not spoil, a useful trick learned from apartment living.

Fastidious as they are about cleanliness–their own persons, food dishes, and surroundings–cats are equally fastidious about the quality and condition of food. If it is not fit to eat, a cat will not touch it. Once I cooked some frozen fish that had been in my freezer for quite a while. I happened to be very fond of it and looked forward hungrily to my dinner. But the first three bites tasted most peculiar, and I began calculating just how long that fish had been in the refrigerator. Longer than it should have been, I decided ruefully, and offered a safety-check taste to Monster. If he ate it, I knew it would be safe for me; but if he turned down an opportunity to feast on fish, I had better do likewise.

It was unfortunate that I had eaten those three bites. Monster sniffed at his sample with a look of disgust and refused to taste it—and I was violently ill for several days.

Outdoor cats and working cats, unfortunately, often fare indifferently. If they are farm cats, they are likely to rely heavily on mice for their protein. The dish of bread and milk (I disapprove of bread because it is starchy) or canned catfood that their well-meaning humans set out for them is supplemental rather than sustaining.

It would take a lot of mice to make eight ounces of meat for each of a dozen cats every day; besides, as a rule, cats kill mice for fun and eat them only through necessity. Furthermore, the hides and tails of rodents are said to be poisonous to cats, and a hard-working mouser needs a good diet to keep his strength at working level.

Working cats, I believe, should be fed enough by their humans so that they need not supplement their diets with wild life. Too often, a mouse may have its remaining hours numbered because it ate some of the poisoned grain scattered around as a pesticide. A poisoned cat comes to a very sad end, paying far too dearly for that last mouse that he would not have eaten had he not been hungry, for a well-fed cat will not usually eat his catch, even though he may kill it. It is as instinctive for cats to chase mice, birds, and bunnies as it is for "sportsmen" to chase birds and animals when "the season is open." Many a cat earns his keep by protecting stores, barns, and warehouses from rats and mice and does his job well because he is properly fed and cared for.

Cats that are allowed outside but are not required to work for their living sometimes pick up a little snack of wild life, but half the time they do not bother to eat it when they have finished playing with it. Mowser, fed regularly by his humans, used to enjoy frog-hunting in his younger days. One of those very rare cats who loves to swim on a hot summer day and insists on going out into a pouring rainstorm, his technique was cleverly designed to make frogging always a successful venture. He would head for the pond and walk slowly over the grass until he came to the brook. Then he would wade through the center of the stream and yowl a warning to all frogs within earshot.

The alarmed frogs instinctively leapt from their siesta places on the bank into the sanctuary of the water where Mowser took his pick, ate it daintily, or—more often—brought it home alive, grinning at his subterfuge.

Even when he was young enough to prowl more than he does now (having had a few bad encounters with animals whose teeth were as sharp as his own), he seldom killed birds or rabbits. Of course, once in a while he came home looking guilty and satisfied with a feather or two still clinging to his whiskers. But it is a neat trick for a cat to capture a healthy bird, because mature birds in flight are five times as fast as cats.

Nevertheless, no one enjoys the possibility of a cat killing the pretty little feathered friends. If you have a cat who lives outdoors part of the time and feel that he is a menace to the bird population, keep him indoors during the nesting season from dusk until eight in the morning. This gives parent birds time to feed and protect their babies unmolested.

Some people put belled collars on their cats to warn the birds, but I think the bells are of questionable value. I have noticed birds around my daughter's summer house very quickly grow accustomed to the bells that Valentina and Marmalade wear, and a couple of times, it was all too evident that the bells had not protected the birds. Also, unless the collar is elastic, the cat is in danger of getting hung up on a shrub, unable to free himself from the caught collar.

I am convinced that the longevity of well-cared-for cats is being extended as greatly as it is in humans because cat-lovers now have no excuse for not feeding their pets a healthful, well-balanced diet. Minnie's eighteenth birthday party last summer may have been nowhere near her last, and I am beginning to believe she is no longer to be considered a freak of old age.

7

The Well-Groomed Cat

Cats who have access to trees and outdoor living have less need of beauty treatments from their humans than do cats who never go outdoors. They can sharpen their claws on tree trunks, loosening the dead nails, and rid their coats of loose, dead fur by rambling through brambles and stiff weeds. They can also dig tidy holes in soft earth in a private spot and neatly cover their excretions.

Indoor cats need to be brushed and to have their nails clipped. They need something to scratch and, of course, a well-tended litter box.

Cats come equipped with claws because they need them. I think I would miss my own fingernails, which serve various useful purposes. So I do not approve of indoor-cat-owners' having a kitten's claws removed in order to protect the furniture. There are other measures that can be taken to prevent furniture damage, for claws are often useful even to an indoor cat, especially when he is eating.

I have seen my cats hold one end of a bone with a firm paw, claws extended, in order to make it easier to gnaw on the other end; without claws, Monster could never have fished out the olives!

Claws show themselves harmlessly in a kneading motion that expresses happiness; claws help a cat keep his balance when he climbs or jumps. They are useful for swift, forward propulsion of any kind, and even a cat without claws is bound to want to move forward or upward in a hurry, more than once a day.

Nevertheless, I must admit that Dr. Roth makes a good point in favor of "de-clawing." When he read this part of my manuscript, he said reasonably, "But sometimes it's a question of de-clawing or destroying the cat." I reared back for battle and thought about how I would probably feel if I had spent the fabulous sums that can be spent on furniture and home decorating, instead of making my own sturdy slip covers, which I *expect* to have shredded. I also had a mental picture of the furniture that my slip covers obscure. So I listened.

"De-clawing," said Dr. Roth, "of course is necessary in the case of pet ocelots and other essentially wild animals. But it's often necessary, too, with just ordinary pet cats. It doesn't hurt them—we give them an anesthetic, and take out only the front claws. And indoor cats don't miss them at all. Naturally, we'd never do it to an outdoor cat—because outdoors, they need their front claws for climbing trees and getting away from other animals. De-clawing is perfectly all right—it really is." I trust Dr. Roth implicitly; but *my* cats can ruin my furniture, what is left of it, if I cannot train them not to!

Nail-clipping, however, is a necessity for indoor cats and an operation that I do not particularly relish. When I hear a little ticking sound as a cat walks across my carpeted floor, I reach for the nail-clippers. The claws have little retrieving hooks on the ends, and when they are in need of clipping, they catch in the threads of the carpet, impeding progress. Without the hooks, the claws are just as useful to the indoor cat and far more comfortable.

If his human does not attend to his nails, the cat will spend hours gnawing at them himself. It is not nervousness that makes a cat bite his nails; comfortable walking is his goal. Yet when I corral the cats for a clipping session, they invariably accuse me of dire intent, squirming and wriggling, making every effort to give me a hard time. I have found the best thing to do is to park myself in a left-hand corner of a chair (I am right-handed), with the cat tucked under my arm, firmly held by my left elbow. Then I gently grasp a forepaw in my left hand, pressing softly on the pad so that the claws protrude.

I use a well-made toenail claw-clipper, the kind that nips when you press down on it, rather than the clippers commercially designed for cat's claws. I am a bit wary of the latter type except in professional hands, because it seems too possible to catch more of the claw than you should if the cat squirms.

In each claw is a tiny pink thread of blood, where a vein extends down toward the end of the claw. It stops short of the hooked claw end and should *never* be cut.

With the toenail-clippers, I nip off just the hook of each claw. It takes a very short time, once I have the cat firmly tucked into a corner, and he feels absolutely nothing except the discomfort of being confined against his will, which in some cats produces panic.

For several reasons, I never cut the back claws myself.

Back feet are jumping and pushing feet, and sometimes the presence of unclipped claws can make the difference between a successful leap and a disastrous flop. The back claws are much sturdier, thicker, and stronger than the front ones, and are difficult to cut. They seem to be blunter on the ends, without the little retrieving catch hooks. The cat uses his back claws frequently for scratching himself to relieve a tickle or remove some real or imaginary foreign particle from his fur. Occasionally, after one of my cats has paid a visit to Dr. Roth, I have noticed that the doctor has clipped *all* the nails—which is the only time my cats get their back nails clipped.

Cats shed the dead tissue of their claws as they grow new bone tissue. If you vacuum your rug every day or so, you may seldom notice the shells of claw, but if you find any, they are no cause for alarm. They are just the outer husks—tiny, translucent-white crescents—and if you give proper attention to the clipping routine, they will seldom have to be shed.

Brushing a cat's coat is much more of a pleasure for him than having his nails trimmed. Monster used to enjoy being brushed so much that he would help me look for the brush and climb happily onto my towel-covered lap whenever it was brushing time. He especially liked to have his stomach brushed and wriggled in glee, curling his paws up and inward, automatically kicking at my brushing hand with his powerful hind legs. I think it tickled him, so—being ticklish myself, I tried not to overdo it.

My favorite brush for cat-grooming is a little plastic vegetable brush that the Fuller man gave me as a free sample years ago. If it ever wears out, I am going to look for one as similar as possible. It has plastic bristles about a half an inch long, which I prefer to the wire brushes made for the purpose, because the teeth cannot possibly tear the cats' fur. Of course, if I had a long-haired cat, I would have to use a stiff, longer-bristled brush. The bristles have to be both flexible and firm, and long enough to reach down to the cat's skin to loosen the shedding hairs and stimulate the healthy flow of blood in the skin.

As cats always love to be scratched on the top of the head, behind the ears, and along the jaw bone to the base of the neck, I begin there, gently brushing back to the tip of the tail. It is fairly common knowledge that most cats strongly dislike having their fur rumpled the wrong way, and even though this procedure would make the brushing task easier, I never sacrifice my cats' pleasure in grooming by this hated method.

It does not take long to brush a short-haired cat's coat, and when the job is done, the cat invariably gives himself a thorough licking. I am sure there is no implied failure on my part of the job. It is merely that once the loose hair has been removed, it makes the cat feel good to lick himself. It is the final polishing that the cat seems to feel only he can do.

Indoor cats need daily brushing, especially in the spring and fall when they shed their unseasonable coats and grow something more comfortable. Long-haired cats need special attention, because sometimes their fur gets matted close to the skin and the brush may tangle, pulling painfully. These little mats have to be patiently teased out with fingers and comb, and occasionally—if the snarl refuses to loosen—must be clipped away with scissors.

I once saw a cat on the street frantically trying to lick away a wad of chewing gum that had become attached to his fur. I hope he lived with a thoughtful human who cut the gum away, for I do not think the cat could accomplish that distressing job alone.

It is seldom necessary or advisable to wash a cat. Most cats do not enjoy the process, and unless they are kept warm for a couple of hours after the bath, they are in danger of catching cold. When the rare need for a bath does arise, the water should be warm (about 90° F.), and if it needs a water softener, borax—not soda—should be added to it. Castile soap is best, because it is pure and unscented. Dunk the cat gently into the water, tail end first, and saturate his body fur from neck to tail with thick lather. Do his head last, mouth and nose up to the ears, then down the back of his head (careful of his eyes!), and rinse him thoroughly in clear water. Dry him immediately in a big, absorbent bath towel, and keep him out of drafts for at least two hours.

There are dry shampoos for cats. I believe a dry shampoo would be preferable to a water bath in most cases. They are powders that you brush through the cat's coat and brush out completely.

Last summer, my cat-friend Alice developed splotches in her fur. They were places where the fur stuck together and caused mats, even though she was a short-haired tabby. Her people took her to the vet, who came up with an interesting diagnosis: Alice, then close to ten years old, was so fat that she could not reach some places for her usual tongue-licking. So the mats had to be cut away, and Alice had to be put on a diet and given more frequent brushing, which she disliked as much as she loved between-meal snacks.

Most cats living indoors all the time spend hours bathing themselves. And Jo-Jo, typical of the altered male in love with his mate, spends hours each day licking SuziTu's coat. SuziTu adores this attention, frequently returning the favor. One night, this loving couple had taken their favorite places on the comfortably warm top of my light-garden cabinet, SuziTu sitting tall and straight with her nose up and eyes closed, while Jo-Jo patiently caressed her throat with his rough little tongue.

Suddenly, Minnie gave voice from the bedroom, and Jo-Jo, as usual, dropped everything to run to the door. SuziTu held her body pose, but looked inquiringly after him as he departed. She resumed her ecstatic expression, eyes closed, nose up, when he came trotting back, after finding the door closed between Minnie and him.

As before, Jo-Jo sat close and tall before SuziTu, but began to lick his own shoulder. SuziTu opened her eyes, her whole body expressing surprise and disbelief, and reached out with a long brown forepaw to tap him on his shoulder. When a second tapping brought no response from him except continued attention to his own toilet, SuziTu resignedly folded herself down beside him and tucked her nose under his soft hip. After all, she seemed to conclude, Jo-Jo was probably entitled to bathe himself, too.

Ear-cleaning is a less-popular sport than brushing, but actually I think most cats enjoy it, even though they pretend not to. In general, a cat's attitude toward grooming and cleanliness seems always to be "I'd rather do it myself!" Ear-cleaning is a very delicate but very important job, to be undertaken calmly and gently and only when necessary. When a cat's ears show black specks deep inside, they must be cleaned or infection can set in. There may be an accumulation of a black, waxy substance, conducive to ear mites, which are live parasites and need a veterinarian's attention.

When Minnie was young, I declared her nitwittedness was manifest because she frequently shook her head rapidly from side to side as though to clear her brain, and a ludicrous rattling noise accompanied the motion. I claimed her brains were rattling. Later, I learned from Dr. Roth that she had an infestation of ear mites, and I had been maligning her. Hearing and being tickled by them made her shake her head, and the "rattling brains" were actually wax in her ears.

I use no tool for ear-cleaning except my fingers and tiny wads of cotton dipped in oil. Mineral oil is recommended, but I never seem to have any when I want it, so I use salad oil. Since it has a vegetable base, it cannot hurt the cat when he does his final licking job. Hydrogen peroxide diluted with warm water is necessary if the neglected ear interior has grown crusty.

One may be tempted to use toothpicks with cotton wrapped around them, or bobby pins. Resist the temptation. I consider them unsafe. The slightest twitch of the cat's head could result in a punctured ear drum. So I take my little wad of oiled cotton and very gently wipe out the ear, reaching as deeply as possible with my finger into every convolution of the outer ear. A fresh wad of cotton after each swipe gets the ear clean in short order.

Actually, I seldom have to clean my cat's ears, but I check them every day just to be sure. Most cats take pretty good care of their own ears, and Jo-Jo seems to be an ear specialist. In his tireless mothering of his kittens, it was he—not SuziTu—who cleaned the babies' ears most often. He would hold the kitten down with a firm paw and run his pointed little tongue into each ear until he was satisfied it was clean. Now that the kittens are gone, he devotes a good bit of attention to SuziTu's ears.

Since cats cannot brush their teeth after each meal, we have to rely on proper diet to keep them clean. The crunchy texture of kibbled food, served dry, is excellent for a mature cat's teeth, and when it is soaked in milk or water, it is good for young and old cats, too.

It is good practice to have the veterinarian check up on the condition of a cat's teeth when the cat is making a visit to him, and especially when the cat is more than five years old. Poor kitty cannot tell you when he has a toothache except by hungrily approaching his food dish, only to sit before it drooling excessively without eating. Then you *know* his teeth are bothering him. It is better to prevent it by having them cleaned when they need it.

A tidy, conveniently located litter box is as essential as the feeding dishes for a cat who never goes out of doors. Cats are notoriously fastidious, and the box has to be kept clean and tidy at all times, both for the cat's sake and for the comfort of the humans who share a home with him. My cats never fail to utilize the facilities as soon as I have changed the box to fresh litter, as though they had saved up their need against a time when appreciation should be expressed. And often, they ask me to follow them to the box so that they can point out the need for a change.

When Monster came to live with us, I used shredded newspaper in his box. I got him an enamelware baking pan, lined it with one double-spread of newspaper, folded down into the corners while the inside surface was wet with fresh water so it would stay put, and tore up another double-spread into short pieces, which I scattered over the lining. When it was time to change the box, it was easy to lift out the lining, fold it over the shredded paper, and dispose of it in the incinerator.

I used the newspaper filler for years, partly because there were then few commercially prepared litters available, and because during the depression, every extra cent of cost in supporting our family had to be calculated carefully.

In recent years (ostensibly more affluent and definitely more lazy), I have used prepared litters. Although I still have the old enamelware pan for a spare if needed, I prefer my new plastic ones. They are flatter on the bottom and give the cat more security in his preoccupation. It is easy to wash them out with hot water and detergent, whereas the old enamelware pan has developed a few chipped places that are difficult to clean. I found no fault with the aluminum pan I used before the plastic ones, except that I had to watch it carefully for possible corrosion. Although I know little about metals, I do know that plastics are smooth until they break apart.

One reason I prefer the plastic pans is that they are about four inches deep and the cats do not scratch litter out of them as readily as they do from shallower pans. A couple of inches of litter in each pan seems to be just about right, and with three cats using two pans, I usually have to change the litter only once a week.

The commercial litters are much more satisfactory than the newspaper filler, especially if there is more than one cat in the house. I have tried almost every commercial litter on the market, I think, and have a definite preference for some brands over others, based on their absorbency and deodorizing properties. They are all made of finely ground clay materials, treated to make them odorless and to dry out rapidly. The enthusiastic manufacturers tell you merely to lift out the solids and add fresh litter as the supply diminishes. But I find it more satisfactory to stir up the contents of the pan a couple of times a day, bringing the more moist lower layer to the surface to dry, as well as lifting out the solids; and once a week, at least, dump the entire contents into newspaper for disposal and thoroughly wash the pan in hot water and detergent before refilling it with all-new litter.

Before the commercial litters became so readily available,

people used to use sand or sawdust in the litter box. Both are difficult to dispose of, track around the house to get ground into rugs and flooring, and could be dangerous to the cat if they got into his eyes.

Once in a while, a cat teaches himself (or his humans teach him) to use the toilet, the bathtub, or the shower drain. His humans usually consider this very clever, but I believe most cats prefer the privacy and comfort of their own facilities which more closely resemble the outdoor arrangements that have been cat tradition for centuries.

One day several years ago, Mowser encountered a skunk. He came home reeking and was promptly ordered to get out and stay out until he smelled clean again. He obediently took off and was gone for several hours. When he returned, there was no trace of skunk odor about him except one faintly scented spot on the very top of his head. It was easy to overlook, since he smelled delightfully of lavender.

Mowser had been for a swim, dried his fur in the sun, and rolled in a bed of fragrant herbs before he presented himself for inspection. The spot on the top of his head was the only spot that had not been dunked during his swim. After all, he had to keep his nose out of water!

Outdoor cats are often subject to this type of unfortunate encounter, and it is a rare cat who really enjoys swimming, as Mowser does. Skunk odor is very difficult to overcome and usually clings for days and days. Even if you could stand the smell long enough to shampoo it out of the cat's fur, I believe it would be safer to phone the veterinarian first for two reasons: It may or may not be safe to use a deodorizing toilet soap on the cat; and the veterinarian may have some other recommendation for deodorizing that will be safer, quicker, and easier.

There is also a danger that the skunk's spray may have got into the cat's eyes, and if there is any indication of this problem—watery eyes, even a runny nose—you will need the doctor's advice.

Apartment cats seldom have fleas unless they go outdoors or have caught fleas before they came to live in the apartment. But Domino, first of my adult-life cats, was an outdoor cat, and somewhere on his prowls through the nearby meadows, he picked up some fleas. I discovered them on one of our trips to Connecticut and hotfooted it to the nearest drugstore to ask what to do about it. The pharmacist sold me a bar of flea soap, and I proceeded to scrub Domino in the laundry tub. It worked, although years later I read in "the book" that one should neither use any kind of medicated soap on a cat nor a flea cure intended for dogs; that derris powder brushed carefully into the coat is the proper cure for fleas; and that vaseline and a fine-tooth comb, plus patience, is an alternative treatment. Nothing the cat cannot safely lick should ever be used.

Outdoor animals are likely to collect ticks in their fur. Ticks are blood-sucking insects that latch onto animal or human, burrow into the skin, swell up, and fill with dark blood. Unless they are removed completely, including the head that is buried in the poor animal's flesh, they can cause serious illness. They are known carriers of Rocky Mountain fever.

To rid a cat of ticks, "the book" recommends a tablespoonful of derris powder dissolved in a gallon of warm water and a cup of mild soap flakes worked up to a lather for a bath. When you have thoroughly washed the afflicted cat with the lather, you leave the soap in the fur, but dry the cat carefully and brush his coat the following day. If there are any ticks that survived this dunking, they have to be removed with tweezers, which is a touchy job. If you jerk them out violently, the head may remain under the skin and fester. And you should wear rubber gloves, just in case the ticks transfer to you.

Turpentine (keep it away from the cat's skin) can be used to kill the ticks once you have pulled them out. They will be easier to remove if you first anesthetize the creatures with a drop of clear acetone (nail-polish remover). But again, do not let the acetone touch the cat.

In ticklish questions of grooming, as in problems of health, when in doubt, ask your vet. Grooming is only partly for beauty's sake.

8

In Sickness and in Health

Cats are almost never sickly. Either they enjoy radiantly good health or they succumb quickly to a desperate illness. Sometimes they have accidents, just as humans do, and sometimes they recover remarkably well—a fact that has given rise to the erroneous theory that a cat has nine lives.

I do not know how many of his "nine lives" were left after Monster fell out of the window, but he did survive a fifty-foot fall and lived another five years afterward. It was not more than six weeks after we had moved from the tiny apartment in which he had always lived, with its two-foot-wide exterior window sills. He had been accustomed to going outside the window in the living room on occasion to sit in the sun. In the new apartment, we had wide window sills, too, but they were in the interior of the apartment, with only a three-inch ledge outside.

Both Minnie and Monnie appeared to adjust readily to the new window-sill locations and enjoyed sitting on them, looking out. One evening when I had guests, Monster disappeared as usual; we could not find him when the guests were ready to bid him good-by. When they had gone, I started a search, calling him, with Minnie worrying at my heels. Finally, I asked, "Minnie, where's Monster?"

She led me to the bedroom window. I looked down, and there, six stories below, was my dear little white friend lying on the grass. I shrieked at him, and he looked up, crying. As fast as the elevator could get me there, I shot downstairs, ran around the building, and picked up the trembling cat. Two people sitting on a nearby bench told me they had almost decided to pick him up and take him home with them. They had heard and watched him for almost an hour.

I stroked him gently, and his fur came off in fistfuls. I carried him back upstairs, trying to reassure him with soft, loving words and gentle caresses that would not injure him if he were hurt. Fortunately, even at that hour (it was late in the evening by then), I was able to reach Dr. Roth by phone. I asked him what to look for, what to do, and why Minnie was snarling at her pal.

Dr. Roth asked if any legs appeared broken, if Monnie's back seemed intact and not painful, and told me to look into his mouth and see if his jaws were in working order. Then, he said, I should watch to see if the poor cat ate normally for the next few days. He added that the reason Minnie was being so uncordial was that she knew Monnie had had an unshared experience, and it frightened her.

As it turned out, Monster suffered nothing but shock and an extremely dirty face. Three days later, it was clean and white again. Apparently, he had plowed into the grassy lawn head on, knocked himself out for a spell, and waked later, lost, stunned, and scared green. In a few days, all the fur came off his left forepaw, leaving a big bald patch with no sign of skin abrasion. Eventually, the fur grew back normally, but twice in subsequent years, the same bald spot appeared. I think perhaps he had been frightened again, either by the memory or a dream of falling, or by too close a call to the possibility of a repeat performance.

For a long time, he would not go near a window again, even though I immediately got screens for every window in the apartment, locking the barn door too late, but making it impossible for such an accident to recur. I will never know how he came to lose his balance, but I have always suspected that he and Minnie were playing tag, chasing each other through the rooms as they so often did, and he forgot about the window sill being in a new place. (Mowser once knocked himself silly when he ran head-on into a recently relocated piece of furniture, too.)

Sabrina, playmate of SuziTu's kitten, Mr. X, fared a bit worse than Monster when she was chasing birds that flew past her second-story window. She fell out and broke a leg, which had to be put into a cast. The story had a happy ending, though. Sabrina was running around as usual two weeks later, having removed her cast when she got tired of being hampered by it.

Anyone who lives with cats in an apartment should always have screens on all the windows that can be opened, winter and summer. It is the only real security against accidents that are often fatal. City-dwelling parents of small children take the simple precautions of installing railings outside their windows to keep the children from falling out. And the same precautions, scaled down to a size that will really protect small animals, are essential for pet-owners. It amounts to criminal negligence not to provide protection against falls for any living creature who is subject to thoughtlessness, carelessness, or ignorance of potential danger. Cats, even more than dogs, are likely to subject themselves to the menace of a fall from a window sill. Monster and Sabrina were both just extraordinarily lucky.

It is almost inevitable that little paws get burned sooner or later. Something that smells wonderful lures the inquiring cat to investigate the top of the range, and blistered paws result. When it happened to Minnie, she lost the skin on both forepaws, although I coated them gently with vaseline to ease the pain by keeping the air out. Patiently and without a complaining sound, Minnie sat out three days with her forepaws upturned, unable to walk on them. Although most of the cats who have lived to maturity with me have discovered that a range top is hot, Minnie suffered most and longest—all in characteristically patient silence.

Minnie's habit of suffering in silence has sometimes misled me. There was the time I was washing paint brushes in turpentine and tipped the bottle over just as Minnie appeared underfoot, getting a blast of the abrasive liquid all over her poor little back. Soundlessly, she ran into the living room, and I thought she was all right. But when she leapt up onto the piano and rubbed herself against the cool sheet music standing on the rack, I knew I had to do something quickly. It was apparently too urgent to waste time on phone calls to the veterinarian or druggist. First aid was of the utmost importance.

So I snatched her up, ran into the bathroom, and dunked her into the washbowl filled with lukewarm water and mild soapy lather. She neither protested nor struggled as I carefully and quickly washed her fur and skin free of the turpentine, dried her thoroughly with a big bath towel, and patted her until her nerves were soothed, apologizing endlessly for having tipped the stuff over onto her. Minnie is so resigned to being clumsy that she has never accused me of hurting her.

I do not take chances with illnesses or accidents by giving my cats the medicines or soothing ointments I would use for myself. When a cat needs medicine, I get it from Dr. Roth, because in so many chemical and medicinal materials that are perfectly safe for humans, there is enough of something poisonous to cats to take all nine lives at once.

For example, one of my dependable reference books says there is enough strychnine in castor oil to kill a cat. Yet another that I would expect to be thoroughly trustworthy recommends castor oil for almost everything. Should I argue the point? I hated castor oil when I was a child, and I would never risk giving it to a cat. Besides, when I discussed the question with Dr. Roth, he remarked, "Castor oil is so outdated, even for humans! Nobody uses it any more." Yet the books that had referred to it were this year's revisions and are currently being circulated as gospel on the care of cats.

Also banned from the list are carbolic acid, DDT, iodine, and all coal-tar by-products.

On the positive side of the medicine cabinet, these are the mild curatives, pain relievers, and first-aid treatments that are harmless to cats: boric acid (for eye wash and cleansing wounds); mineral oil, olive oil, cod-liver oil (for internal and ear lubrication); hydrogen peroxide for softening crusted wax in the ears; milk of magnesia; salt or epsom salts if you need to make the cat vomit a poison; aspirin if you need to keep him comatose until the veterinarian arrives, as in the case of convulsions; a few (four or five) drops of brandy or whisky, if he needs a little boost. *Nothing* else out of your medicine cabinet should be given to a cat unless his doctor recommends it, and these only in prescribed doses.

For scrubbed-clean accessories, baking soda, salt and water, or a weak solution of chlorox are acceptable, but keep the chlorox away from the cats, and rinse and rinse and rinse so there will be no residue.

When Minnie began making frequent trips to the litter box and passing only very small quantities of bloody urine, I rushed her off to Dr. Roth, who diagnosed her problem as cystitis, inflammation of the bladder sometimes caused by a cold. He gave me large purple pills to feed her. He also assured me that although cystitis in a male cat is almost guaranteed to be fatal (in fact, it was Monster's last illness), a female cat with cystitis suffers nothing more serious than slight discomfort and can live happily for a long time. The purple pills should help it, he said, so I diligently proceeded to stuff purple pills into Minnie's mouth four times a day. (This was ten or twelve years ago, and Minnie is healthy at eighteen.)

Feeding Minnie pills was an accomplishment that proved to be a neat trick, requiring some dexterity, since Minnie took a dim view of the whole idea and refused to be tricked by the favored technique of burying a pill in her food.

So four times a day I covered my lap with a towel, swathed Minnie in it, held her firmly, and opened her tightly clenched jaws. To get her to open her mouth even in protest was an impossibility. The only safe way to force a cat's mouth open is to put your hand behind her head, place your thumb on one side and your middle finger or forefinger on the other at the jaw hinges, and gently but firmly press inward until the mouth opens. Then, with the other hand, you have to pop the pill in, way at the back of the tongue so it will not come spitting out, release the jaw pressure, hold her mouth closed with the grasping hand, stroke her throat with the other one until she swallows, and then let her jump down off your lap, turn around to glare at you, and get well in self-defense. Sounds easy?

I became quite adept at it after a while, because it took a lot of pills to relieve her ailment. I must admit that, in time, she became a bit more docile about the whole thing, learning that if she did not put up too much of a fight, it would all be over in half a minute, and that since the pill administration was something from which I was not to be thwarted, she might as well give in gracefully.

Giving liquid medicine is another trick, not much easier than the pill procedure. I had to learn it when Monster was feeling poorly after his worming session. Not all cats have worms. In fact, Monnie is the only one I have known who did. I learned that they come from fleas (which are hosts to tapeworms) and sometimes are inherited from the mother cat. Monnie had a tapeworm that became evident, to my horror, when he was still quite young. Little white rice-grain segments clung to his stool, so off he went to Dr. Roth for treatment.

Returning home after whatever emetic siege he had had, Monnie no longer had worms, but neither did he have his normal healthy attitude and appetite. He moped and looked dreary, put-upon, and sad. Again I called Dr. Roth for advice. "Give him four drops of brandy three times a day," advised my mentor.

So I hied me to a liquor store and asked for a small bottle of brandy suitable for a cat; to a drugstore for a medicine dropper; and back home to treat my unsuspecting friend to a big surprise. Having loaded the medicine dropper on the theory that four short squirts would produce four drops of brandy, I lured my trusting little Monster onto my lap. I stroked his head gently and felt like a heel because he adored the attention. He opened his mouth in a happy grin, and I shot the medicine dropper into it, aiming at his cheek pocket, as the book said, so as not to choke him. Startled, he shook his head. Equally startled, I squeezed the dropper bulb, and a full twenty or thirty drops of brandy went hotly down his throat.

Monnie leapt to the floor, throwing me a baleful look over his shoulder. He shook his head, then with a double-take expression, licked his lips. Weaving a little, he came back to my chair, climbed up onto my lap, and promptly fell asleep. It took him two hours to sleep off his jag, but when he awoke, he was his normal, peppy self—hungry, alert, and happy. I had to find other uses for the rest of the brandy.

Now I know that the four drops of brandy should have been administered each time *in a dropperful of milk!*

Just in case the tapeworm affliction should recur, I decided I should give Monster what the book recommended as the best worm-preventer—minced garlic. He loved it. I put about a teaspoonful in his food, and he thought it was great—until his dignity got involved.

One night my across-the-hall neighbors and I went to the movies. When we came home, we opened my door before saying goodnight. A wave of garlic followed by a happy Monster came to greet us, and we all burst into hearty guffaws. "Oh, Monster!" we howled. "The way you smell!" Monster never touched garlic again, nor did he ever have any more worms.

There is no "slight" illness in a cat. Either the cat is vibrantly well, or he is at death's door; and on the few occasions when one of my cats has acted sick, I have wasted no time in getting proper medical help. I lost my dear little Suzanne only because it was impossible on that Saturday night when she was sick to find a veterinarian, known or unknown, to treat her.

It was obvious that she had been poisoned. Apparently in the best of health one moment, in the next she suddenly began to vomit a horrible-smelling, foamy, yellow-green fluid, torrentially and in abject misery. Had I taken her temperature, I am sure it would have been well above the normal 101½ degrees.

Frantically, I phoned first Dr. Roth's office, then one unknown vet after another, including the city's small-animal hospital to no avail. Within a few hours, the poor little body looked as though she had been sick for weeks—thin, dull-eyed, dull-coated. Before morning, she stretched out under my bed and went to her final sleep.

What poisoned her? She had exactly the same food as she was accustomed to, and shared it with Minnie and Jo-Jo, neither of whom was sick. It was several days before I discovered her killer. On the bathroom floor near the litter box was a dried bittersweet berry, fallen from a pretty little arrangement I had carefully placed on a high corner shelf, out of cats' reach, because I knew that bittersweet of the deadly nightshade family is poisonous to cats. It must have started to shed its berries, even though I had sprayed it with clear plastic to hold them on their stems. Loving to nibble anything in the berry line, Suzanne must have found and eaten one.

Pretty as bittersweet is for autumn color in an apartment, I now leave it in its native outdoors. Suzanne, so full of life and grace and sweetness, was too high a price to pay for a touch of decorative color on a shelf.

My inability to get medical help at that time led to locking another barn door too late. Naturally, in the early days of living with a cat, his human chooses a well-recommended veterinarian who knows and likes cats and sticks to him like a brother. The doctor's phone number is posted where anyone can find it readily in emergency, and his address (preferably a nearby location) is listed with it. But I had neglected to add to this information a number where I might reach Dr. Roth after office hours, and Suzanne's poisoning occurred on a weekend. Such small, unthinking mistakes like that depress the thoughtful human who loves his pets!

Recently, I called the New York Botanical Gardens to ask what other popular house plants might be injurious to cats and was surprised to learn that the Jerusalem Cherry is another member of the deadly nightshade family, and therefore equally poisonous. Solanum, tobacco, jimson weed, mistletoe berries, henbane, and matrimony vine are other plants that could be harmful if eaten, and of course, diffenbachia (dumb-cane), although it is doubtful that a cat would eat it because of its texture.

When a cat has been poisoned, send for the vet and administer first aid while you wait. Poisoning can be caused, as in Suzanne's case, by unwitting carelessness with such common household items as decorations or with cleansers. Phenol poisoning, for example, can be caused by some of the cleansers we are most accustomed to using. If you wash the cat's litter pan or the kitchen floor with anything containing carbolic acid, creolin, creosote, or lysol, you are endangering the cat's life, because their basic chemicals are deadly to felines. These same ingredients are also found in many common disinfectants, so read the labels carefully.

First-aid treatment for most poisons is two teaspoonfuls of milk of magnesia or epsom salts in a little warm water; or a teaspoonful of salt, placed on the back of the cat's tongue to make him vomit. If it is strychnine poisoning, there is very little hope that anything can be done to save the cat from swift and terrible death, but when you see its first indications—shaking and twitching of the cat's body that can quickly develop into convulsions—make him vomit if at all possible. (Convulsions *must* be prevented.) When he has done so, immediately give him a five-grain aspirin tablet. If the twitching continues, give him another half tablet; and if necessary, another whole one. A mature cat can stand up to three tablets of aspirin, and it seems to be the only readily available remedy that can prevent convulsions. It may make the cat unconscious, but at least the poor little animal will be out of his misery for a time, until the doctor can treat him.

Poisoning from phosphorus, phenol, arsenic, or lead (the latter is sometimes caused by paint or paint fumes) shows itself by violent vomiting of a greenish fluid, such as Suzanne experienced. A dose of milk of magnesia might have saved her, but she needed a doctor in a hurry.

Suzanne's brother, Josephus, came to an untimely end less than a year before she died. I should have noticed sooner that something was wrong with Joey's ear, but the swelling was on the inside at first, and at that time I was not so conscious as I am now of the need for daily checking inside the cats' ears. Too, his normal joyous attitude deceived me until one morning, as he sat on my chest inviting me to get up and serve breakfast, I noticed for the first time that his ear lopped grotesquely to one side.

I put on my glasses and examined the drooping ear closely. There was a huge lump inside it, so gross that it distorted the shape of his head. Immediately, we went to Dr. Roth, who said that it was an abscess that must be operated on promptly. I left Joey at the hospital, and when I brought him home a few days later, he seemed dejected and had no appetite.

Knowing that food should not be forced on a sick cat, I dug out my medicine dropper, mixed a raw egg with milk and a few drops of whisky, and fed it to the dispirited little animal. Still he did not perk up. His coat was dull, his eyes sad, and I knew he was a really sick cat.

As luck would have it, transportation in New York was paralyzed that day by one of those rare snowstorms. By the time it was possible for me to find a cab to take Joey back to the hospital, he was beyond saving. "He's a very sick little fella," Dr. Roth said seriously. "I'll do what I can for him, but I can't promise anything."

Utterly miserable, I went home to wait for Dr. Roth's report. About three hours later, I suddenly knew that I would never see Joey again. I rushed to the phone and called the hospital. "I was just about to call you," said Dr. Roth sadly. . . .

I do not know what killed Joey. The symptoms were those of feline enteritis, which is terribly contagious and almost always fatal. It kills within forty-eight hours of its inception. Neither Minnie nor Suzanne came down with it, so obviously it was not enteritis. There are some other feline diseases that are not so infectious, but have closely similar symptoms.

Infectious enteritis (also known as feline distemper, malignant panleukopenia, and infectious feline agranulocytosis) is one of the two most dread diseases to which cats are susceptible. The other is feline pneumonitis. Once either disease has entered your household, you should not even associate with another cat for at least six months. *You* can spread it, carrying the virus on your shoes or other clothing. Both diseases can be prevented by having the veterinarian give the cat preventive injections, and kittens should never be deprived of their "shots" once they have been weaned.

Sometimes, however, before the little ones are old enough to leave their mother, feline enteritis creeps in to do its dirty work among them. This is what happened when Chieng Jo-Jo was still being nursed by his mother, Leing. Somehow Leing came in contact with cat or human who carried the dread virus, contracted enteritis, and passed it along to all of her kittens, as well as to her mate, Chieng Ho-Ho. Ho-Ho and Leing both survived, having undoubtedly been inoculated when they were younger. Of the kittens, only Jo-Jo survived.

Cats who have once lived through enteritis are said to be immune to it thereafter, but may suffer side effects. A knowledgeable cat-fancier who came to consider purchasing one of SuziTu's first kittens told me something that Dr. Roth has since confirmed as being possible. She admired Jo-Jo even more than his offspring, and to make her feel less unhappy that she could not buy him for love or money, I pointed out his slight hind-quarters' stiffness.

"Oh," she said, "he must have had enteritis sometime when he was a kitten."

Adult cats as well as kittens can be vaccinated for enteritis, and the veterinarian will be able to tell you the best time to do it. Two injections, spaced a week to ten days apart, are usually effective, but if they are given after the cat has already been exposed to the disease, he may contract it.

When they were kitten-hunting last spring, Anne and Kurt adopted Valentina and Marmalade from the Bide-A-Wee shelter in New York, and took them back to the Bide-A-Wee clinic for their first shots a short time later. They were just leaving the doctor's office when Marmalade,

Anne's favorite, suddenly went into convulsions and died. The doctor explained that Marmalade had obviously been allergic to the vaccine, which fortunately is a rare occurrence. There is no way of predicting this rare allergy and no antidote for it.

Infections can be caused by bites as well as by invisible viruses. During the last fight that Minnie provoked Jo-Jo into, he got his teeth into her quite literally, causing her to limp painfully for a couple of days until the lump on her foreleg broke and the infection drained out. If her injured paw had not responded so quickly to her own ministrations, I should have bandaged it with a boric-acid poultice. And if that had not worked, Dr. Roth might have applied one of the "miracle drugs," which, administered professionally, have proved a tremendous boon in pulling back sick and injured cats from death's door. I cannot too often reiterate my belief that a true cat-lover leaves the diagnosis and the cure of anything that is not completely obvious, such as a brief head cold, to the experience and training of a good veterinarian.

And even a cold can be serious, because it may turn out to be that other dread disease, feline pneumonitis. If your cat catches cold, the symptoms will be the same as you have when you catch cold. His nose will run, and he will cough, feel obviously miserable, and not eat. His eyes will water, and he will sneeze. Give him two days in which to show marked improvement under your tender ministrations, and if he is not over it by then, take him to the doctor to see if something more drastic than loving care and plenty of paper hankies is called for. Should it be diagnosed as pneumonitis, the symptoms might last for a month or more unless the cat has proper care, and although most cats recover from pneumonitis in about four weeks, there is a dangerous possibility that an infected cat will die of malnutrition due to his lack of appetite combined with the disease.

Jo-Jo's limp, if you can call it that, did not become apparent until he was about six months old. At least, I passed it off as poor coordination. He has no problem in walking, running straight ahead, or even in making a wide curve. But like a trailer truck, he has to get his hind quarters properly aligned behind his front end before he can proceed normally. The difficulty is apparent when he wants to make an abrupt turn and sometimes when he gets to his feet from a prone position.

When I finally had to admit that his gait is a bit peculiar, that he has to make careful calculations before he leaps from a low place to a higher one, and that although he runs well, he walks with unusual dignity, I worried. Was he in pain? Checking up, it seemed evident that his stiffness is only an inconvenience, and he has accepted philosophically the limitations imposed on him.

Nevertheless, I guiltily recognize the possibility that I may have been responsible for that stiffness. Shortly after I trimmed his nails for the first time, he tried to jump from the floor to the kitchen counter. Although he latched onto the metal strip that borders the counter edge, he did not have enough impetus to keep on going upward. He fell heavily back onto his little rear end and never made the attempt again. Whether unclipped claws would have made his leap successful is an unanswerable question, but I still feel guilty about it.

He has always cringed fearfully when anything—especially a hand or a foot descending the stairs—appears to be lowering itself onto his head; and now that we have stairs to climb, I am more than ever conscious of it. Possibly he was stepped on in his very early kittenhood by one of the little boys in his initial family. I respect his fears and take every precaution not to alarm him, stooping down to his level when I want to pet him or picking him up into my arms when he asks for me to love him for a moment.

I have not had SuziTu spayed, although I know it might be considered unfair to her to leave her unaltered now that Jo-Jo cannot mate with her. Spaying is a more serious operation than castration of a male and requires leaving her majesty in the hospital at least overnight, perhaps longer. Her ovaries are completely removed by making an incision in the abdomen, which of course must be allowed to heal without interference or physical strain from overactivity. Only a thoroughly reliable veterinarian should be entrusted with this delicate job, which cannot be done while the cat is in heat, nor should it be attempted before she is six months old. (I have heard of a spayed female who allegedly developed a tumor as a result of the operation, but this is not a frequent result of spaying.)

Although there is an unfounded theory that neutering makes cats grow fat, it has been my observation that a spayed female, as she gets on in years, develops a loose pouch under her abdomen. I have been told that this pouchiness does not develop if the neutering was done after she had mothered a litter or two.

I do not believe that neutering makes cats fat. They grow fat only from overeating and lack of exercise. But they do, I know, often grow a little larger than they would if they were not altered; and neutering does make them affectionate, soft-spoken, and perhaps more tractable. It does not in the least change either cat's attitude toward his mate. If they loved each other before they were altered, they will continue to love each other afterward.

Anne's Valentina and Marmalade II have both been altered now, and if anything, Valentina seems even more feminine and Marmalade even more boisterously a tom than before their operations. Neither had yet developed a mating urge when they were neutered, so they have no idea of what they missed. But as I mentioned, Minnie was in heat when she came to us, and her subsequent alteration certainly made no difference in the love affair she and Monster spread over their twelve years together.

A few months ago, one of my young friends told me she wanted a kitten and asked how to find one. I talked her into adopting two instead of one and steered her to the American Feline Society. The Society's volunteer case workers put her in touch with a lady who rescues homeless cats, and Vicki was delighted with her month-old babies.

About six weeks later, however, Vicki told me there was something terribly wrong with both kittens' little legs. Walking seemed painful to them; they frequently fell over and were unable to jump or run at all. I was baffled and recommended professional diagnosis, the sooner the better.

Dr. Roth examined the babies, diagnosed their problem as rickets, and gave Vicki the necessary medicines and diet instructions. Although he offered no guarantee that they would recover, it was not more than two weeks before the kittens were romping and playing on sturdy little underpinnings again. It was then that Vicki, puzzled and relieved, mentioned that the "cat-lady" had told her, "Don't feed them milk; it gives them diarrhea."

How can a well-intentioned cat-rescuer be so ignorant? Those kittens, only a month old, should still have been living on their mother's milk. Deprived of that, they naturally needed plenty of fresh or canned milk to build sturdy bones and teeth, just as human children do. They responded quickly to supplementary calcium and reportedly have a corner on the milk market. Foundling kittens often have lost their mother, have no one to feed them milk, and consequently are subject to the crippling effects of rickets. Because Vicki's were still so young, they will be all right, thanks to prompt medical attention.

There are some things that can happen to cats that have not happened to any of mine (knock on wood) and for which an ordinary human with loving intelligence can treat his pet. I do not intend to lure any cat-loving reader into the false sense of security offered by a book that "tells you everything" about how to take care of a cat's health. But there is need for general knowledge of first aid and how to avoid making a nuisance of yourself in your veterinarian's office. Beyond that, my advice will always be "consult your doctor if you have anything unusual to deal with."

For example, if a cat develops a lump, it may be a tumor—benign or malignant—and only the doctor can tell you. If a skin disease makes its appearance—indicated by loss of fur and little blisters that the cat scratches—do not fool around with it.

But if the cat is constipated, you can take emergency care of him yourself with a dose of salad oil, mineral oil, or a meal of raw liver. Do not *ever* give a cat a laxative other than oil or raw liver unless his doctor prescribes it. Laxatives intended for humans can be fatal to cats.

Kittens, even more than adult cats, may have diarrhea. Watch it carefully. It may be caused only by the change from mother's milk to cow's milk; or it may be a symptom of something more serious than a sudden reaction to change in diet. If it lasts more than a day or two, despite a meal of thoroughly cooked liver, check with the doctor.

People who live in snake-infested country should naturally have snake-bite antidotes always at hand. In addition to knowing how and when to use it for humans, they should also know exactly how much serum to give to a snake-bitten cat and how to administer it. There might not be time to get to the cat hospital before the antidote is needed, and cats catch many a snake.

Before I wind up this somewhat depressing discussion of the things that occasionally happen to pet cats, I must mention the one that may alarm the uninitiated, but should cause no worry whatever.

Sometimes a cat woopses up his dinner. Sometimes, too, he retches noisily and finally produces a small quantity of spittle and a blob of fur. This type of vomiting is very different from the poison-caused gushing of greenish-yellow fluid, which seldom seems to contain solids at all.

A cat who has eaten too fast for his digestive system; or to whom you have given a too-cold meal straight out of the refrigerator; or a perfectly good food that just does not agree with him—is likely to bring it back up again because his stomach cannot take it. Since it was probably your fault, all you can do is clean up the mess, tell him you are sorry, and try not to cause him the same discomfort again. In this kind of vomiting, the cat is not sick. Immediately after he has got rid of his problem, he will frisk around as usual and feel fine. He may even go back to his dish for a refill.

The blob of fur, too, is something you can avoid and should apologize for causing. If you brush your cat often and thoroughly, when he licks his fur there will probably not be much that is loose enough to clog his intestines and form a hair ball. If you neglect his grooming and leave it entirely to his own innate sense of cleanliness and tidiness, the loose fur that he swallows will inevitably form a ball, quite possibly cause constipation, and have to come up the way it went down if the mineral oil does not work. It is as simple as that, and you do not have to clean up an unnecessary mess if you brush the cat regularly.

There are numerous excellent books on cat care, some of which are published by the makers of cat foods and medicines and may be available from your veterinarian's office. It is wise to have at least one or two reliable ones on your reference shelf. Most cats are healthy all their lives if their people treat them with intelligence, but when you need a guide, it is good to have a book to rely on.

Everyone knows the one thing that is as inevitable as taxes. Sometimes nature takes care of it when a cat has lived his life out; sometimes his human must make that difficult decision with the help of the veterinarian. Euthanasia, not allowed by allegedly civilized humans among themselves, is perversely considered humane when it is applied to animals.

When Jo-Jo and Minnie began their feud, some of my friends suggested that Minnie's time had come. "After all," they argued, "she's a very old cat."

"She deserves to live out her life," I retorted, "and even if it means a bit of inconvenience for me, I shall see to it that she lives as long and as comfortably as she can and wants to." Would we do away with every sweet little old lady who got so old that she needed care, and who was sometimes irritable?

A few months ago, when Alice's people became alarmed at her failure to eat and function normally, their veterinarian's examination revealed a large intestinal tumor and an alarming degree of anemia. The doctor said it would take some time to correct the anemia sufficiently to allow for an operation, and he recommended that she be put to sleep.

Hearing of this diagnosis, I suggested she should at least

be given a chance at survival, citing that Queenie, my magnificent blue-eyed Angora friend on the farm, had twice had tumors removed successfully and was then alive at the age of sixteen years, whereas Alice was only ten. When the operation was finally performed, Alice's tumor proved to be malignant, and she never was allowed to come out of the anesthetic; but at least her people knew they had given her the chance she deserved.

When it is necessary beyond the shadow of a doubt to put a cat out of pain and misery, it should be done professionally by a sympathetic veterinarian. It is a sad time indeed, and the bereaved human can console himself only with the memories of having shared whatever time was allotted to his friend.

9

Rules of the Game

When cats and people live together, there naturally have to be some rules of the game. If you set up rules that the cat considers reasonable, they will usually be followed except when the cat wants to tease or punish. If the rules are unreasonable in the cat's mind, they will be patently disobeyed from the very beginning, and the cat is likely to go out of his way to point up his disapproval of the unfair regulation.

Some of my friends think me overindulgent with my cats. They say I spoil them by allowing behavior that should be forbidden. But in bringing up my cats, I have followed a pattern of permitting minor transgressions that may annoy or inconvenience me a little, but actually hurt no one, so that when I must say a firm "No," it has meaning and gets the desired reaction. This system works well for me. Most of my rules are based on safety and comfort—theirs as well as mine.

Just do something of which a cat disapproves, and you are in for it! Before Minnie came to live with us, Anne and I used to leave Monnie alone for the weekend while we went to visit in the country. He had plenty to eat and drink, all the comforts of home while we were gone, except companionship. His resentment was strong.

We lived then in a little apartment that had a rather long hall leading from the doorway to a funny-shaped living room, beyond which was a tiny foyer separating the bedroom on one side from the bath on the other. I think there was never a weekend away when we did not return to an utter madhouse of torn-up paper, strewn from the farthest points in the bedroom and the bath straight through the living room to the door. Monnie was showing his disapproval by littering expansively. I suppose I could have frustrated his revenge by hiding the john paper before we left the apartment, but heaven only knows what else he might have found as a tool of expression! I let well enough alone, and he stopped this annoying game when Minnie came, which was influential in confirming me in my two-cat theory.

Minnie's favorite form of expressing disapproval was always the same: piddling in the wrong place. When Anne was a teen-ager, Minnie found more fault with her than even I did. It was not an infrequent occurrence to find Anne muttering bitterly as she stripped her bed, which Minnie quite deliberately had soaked right through to the mattress. Taking a cue from this wicked practice, when Anne went away to college, I covered my own bed with a sturdy plastic bedspread, lest Minnie get vengeful ideas toward me, now that she had lost her prize victim. I have had no such trouble since.

Despite their altered conditions, Monnie remained all male

in his attitude, and Minnie, all female. She still *is* all female, even in her extreme old age. It may have been her femininity —or playing a feminine role—that caused her to behave like a real nitwit. Or it may have been only the contrast with Monnie's extremely active intellect. But aside from apparent slow-wittedness, Minnie was physically the clumsiest cat I ever knew. She watched Monnie leap lightly up onto the bookcase with my precious Wedgwood collection, pick his way among the fragile pieces, and jump down without ever disturbing a thing. Wisely, she did not attempt it after the first time, when she broke a little pitcher. She watched him jump from the floor to the step-stool to the drainboard of the sink and walk along the edge of the sink to the counter on the other side. She tried to follow suit and landed in the dish drain, which fortunately was otherwise unoccupied at the time.

She fell into the bathtub when it was full of water. She sat on an ash tray that contained a lighted cigarette, and I had to put out the fire on her tail. A startled "Hmm-m-m?" was her comment as I splashed water on the conflagration, for apparently smoldering fur made no impression on her, even when it was her fur, but water was not to be tolerated.

She was blandly, innocently, stupidly clumsy. And Monnie took it upon himself, without my asking him, to teach her to do the things that he could do. As usual, communication was mostly silent. Occasionally, he would make an encouraging little crooning sound at her, but mostly he would stare at her for a long minute, then do his trick, then stare at her again until she attempted to imitate him. And teach her he did. He even instructed her in his own self-taught trick of retrieving a little jack ball, and they played together until she knew the trick thoroughly. The odd part of that lesson, though, was that when slow-witted Minnie-the-clumsy-foot finally learned to retrieve, Monnie lost interest in the game.

I love to see a cat smile almost as much as a kitten laugh. Without any change in the expression of his mouth, a cat can smile with his eyes. Monnie used to do it often, especially when I smiled at him. And it was Monnie who started the winking game. Sitting solemnly before me, his golden eyes round and wide open, he would slowly close and open one of them. He would keep it up as long as I cooperated; eventually Minnie tried to do it, but she never learned to close only one at a time. So there we would be, Monnie and Minnie sitting squarely before me, Monnie winking one eye, Minnie winking both, until we all started to laugh, and the game broke up.

Initiating the two-cat system is an experience. Getting an established cat to accept a newcomer requires tact of the humans involved—tact, understanding, and caution. It usually requires about three days, except when it is love at first sight, as in the cases of Monnie and Minnie, Jo-Jo and SuziTu.

No king or queen of the realm is going to take happily to the idea that his or her human has a new love, no matter how much sales pitch you put into the build-up when you introduce the new cat to the established one. This is *his* territory, *his* human. Who is this new upstart who wants to use his litter box, eat at the same feeding station, and sleep on his human's bed?

So the two cats have to work out their own terms by themselves. This may be difficult to arrange, because the newly transplanted cat has his own adjustments to make—explorations, wariness, homesickness, a temporary feeling of insecurity, and such.

Thus the newcomer is trapped in a strange place that is

full of hostility augmented by his own fear. He will tuck himself into the most inaccessible place he can find and lie low in abject misery until he has talked it out with the established ruler. There is absolutely nothing the most understanding human can do about this introductory period except make sure that the outraged, established cat feels secure in his human's affection and cannot hurt the miserably unhappy newcomer while they set up free communication with each other.

The best practice, if you can possibly arrange it, is to put a strong wire screen between the two cats. Not a cage, for it is frightening and too confining. A firmly screened open doorway between two rooms is ideal. They will hiss and swear at each other for a while, and then call a truce, at which point the barrier has served its purpose. Within three days (I have checked it time and again), they will be playing happily together, especially if they are of opposite sexes. The questions of who is boss in charge of what and whom have then been settled. Each knows his role in the family picture. The newcomer has been allowed to explore, aided and even encouraged by his new friend; and together they can plot more trouble than either alone could possibly devise.

When Anne's first little yellow tabby kitten, Marmalade, died so suddenly, she was determined to replace him only with another yellow kitten. It took more than a month to find one, and he turned up for us at the Westport Humane Society on Easter weekend. Valentina had been left alone with a cat-sitter in New York that weekend, so Marmalade II had a chance to get acquainted with his humans before meeting Valentina.

Apparently a healthy, happy kitten, full of love and frolic, Marmalade II worried us by not eating at all after we took him from the shelter, and when we returned to the city on

Sunday evening, I volunteered to spend the following day at Anne's apartment so I could take him to Dr. Roth if he still did not eat or drink. This served also to provide chaperonage while Valentina decided whether or not she was going to like the newcomer.

I woke the next morning with the answer to the eating problem: Marmalade was not weaned. To put him out for adoption at Easter-rush time, his people had taken him from his mother before he had learned to eat from a dish. So I spent most of the day introducing the kitten to the eating process, and to Valentina, who hissed and growled and arched her back, but watched us curiously as I dipped a finger into milk, put it into Marmalade's mouth, and gradually, repeating the process over and over, lowered the finger into the dish and watched him take his first sip without aid.

When he had caught up on nourishment, I kept him where Valentina could not harm him, but could get acquainted gradually. As I petted him, I noticed black spots in his ears. I carefully swabbed them out with salad oil, and Valentina promptly took him in charge. She licked his well-oiled ears until I thought she would rub them off his head. Then the two kittens started romping and playing like old friends. The three-day adjustment period was telescoped into a few hours.

The experienced human, nevertheless, remains a bit wary for a while, especially if he is introducing a young cat to an old one. Minnie had been a widow just long enough to begin to feel her oats as my sole possessor when the kittens, Joey and Suzanne, arrived. I praised Minnie for all sorts of things, so that she would not feel I was displacing her; and I took her to bed with me, shut the door, and left the poor little ones alone in the living room, where they crouched in close entanglement all night. It took Minnie the usual three full days to stop hissing. I kept them apart from her, and they cooperated most willingly, although they occasionally opened their little faces into tiny hissing triangles when they were at a safe distance. Gradually, all tails became normal size, all backs regained normally arched formation, and—the final gesture of acceptance—everybody could eat safely together.

Minnie's acceptance, however, was a surface thing, and her punishment ran true to form. Knowing the one act that would never be tolerated, she snidely proceeded to indoctrinate those innocent babies into an evil practice that was certain to get them into trouble. Only I caught her at it.

As I entered the apartment one evening, Minnie and her pupils were so intent on the lesson she was giving them that they did not hear me close the door. Minnie had the two kittens corralled on the opposite side of the living room, squatting on the edge of the rug. All three of them were piddling.

"Minnie!" I roared, knowing immediately what was going on and why. She leapt up, took a frightened glance over her shoulder at me, and ran for the bedroom, guilt hanging over her like a black halo. The poor kittens caught on fast. They never again mistook the edge of the rug for their box, *except* when I roared at them about some misdemeanor. Then, inevitably, in startled silence, they proceeded purposefully to the rug edge. I finally had to throw the rug away. Once a cat has piddled anywhere, it becomes a place to do it again, right or wrong, unless you can eliminate the odor that only they can detect, which is very difficult to do.

Years ago, it was customary to sprinkle pepper on the rug where a cat mistakenly piddled, and then rub his nose in it. This was not only cruel, but an ineffectual approach to the problem. Today, there are commercial preparations—powders and sprays—that are supposed to smell utterly repulsive to cats, but have no odor for humans. Maybe *some* cats dislike them, but Minnie and her trainees ignored them completely. Very recently, I was told that white vinegar will kill the odor if a cat has made a mistake and can be used to break the habit. Unregrettably, my present cats have given me no opportunity to try it.

Getting acquainted with people is almost as touchy a problem for the cat as getting acquainted with another feline. It is complicated because so many people do not understand the protocol of greeting a strange cat and take offense (or fright) if you try to suggest that they take it easy. A cat is a formal creature who wants always to make the first gesture and only in his own good time.

Kittens especially seem to feel very little need of new people. The humans who were there when the kittens were born and began to grow up are the only people they know, as a rule, and are quite sufficient humanity if they meet the simple requirements of the very young for shelter, love, and comfort.

So when a kitten (or a cat) is transplanted into a new home, his supersensitive little nostrils and his supersensitive little ears are assailed by myriads of strange scents and sounds. New places to explore are fun for any cat, but if he was "born in love," as Dr. Roth recommends, he was born into a take-it-for-granted sense of security and needs far more loving attention from his new owners than did our pickup, Domino, who seemed to have nothing to lose.

One poignant illustration of this adjustment period is that of Jennie. The one kitten of SuziTu's first litter who stood out as different, she was the one of that litter for whom I had a name—and a troublesomely deep affection. The evening appointed for a sure sale of a kitten found me putting on fresh lipstick, seizing Jennie, and kissing her soundly on the top of her little white head. The customer, I knew, was a college boy studying to be a veterinarian. If he chose my lipsticked kitten and I had any doubts about how they would get on together, I would invent a reason why he would much prefer one of the other babies.

"I don't know what my roommates will say—they don't like cats anyhow—when I bring home one with *lipstick* on her!" was Arnold's mild comment as he tucked little Jennie into his zipped-up jacket with my blessing. It had been Jennie from the start, and I knew they would make a good combination—and he will be a good small-animal doctor. So I warned him that, even though Jennie had stood out from the others as an independent, it would take a few days for her to adjust to being a lone cat. She was leaving three littermates, her mother, her father, and me.

A few evenings later, Arnold phoned me, the dismal unhappiness in his voice echoed by a treble feline voice that I recognized. "She plays a little bit," he said, "and then she cries; and then plays a bit more . . . but she cries. What's wrong with her?"

"She's lonely," I replied, hearing her little voice clearly in the background. "What you need is another of her littermates to keep her company."

"That's impossible," he said flatly.

"Then love her, Arnold—just love her." It worked. They are devoted and happy according to latest reports.

Well-meaning people who pounce gleefully on a strange cat (or even on one they know) only get rebuffed. Whenever I meet someone else's cat, whether for the first or the umpteenth time, I greet him cordially and quietly by name, if I know it. I put as much reserve and dignity and cordial respect as possible into my tone without sounding phony—

because a cat knows when he is being talked-down to and resents it wholeheartedly.

If he approaches me, I extend a hand slightly toward him, not too high above his nose, so he can sniff at it. If he does not care to sniff my fingers just then, I withdraw the hand —not suddenly, just put it somewhere else, find something else to do with it—smile pleasantly at him, and turn away. When he is quite ready, he will come to me. He may never be ready, but he most certainly will not be influenced by coaxing, "Here kitty, come to me."

Occasionally, but not often, a cat will take to a stranger as though he were a long-lost brother, and as soon as the human is seated, will rub against his ankles or even leap into his lap, settling down happily for a little cozy communion. The appropriate thing to do at this point is to stroke the cat's head gently, behind the ears and under his chin, but not to confine him in a bear hug or start to maul and fiddle with him.

Some cats are not lap cats at all, ever. Some are lap cats from kittenhood. And some prefer to share a seat, nestling close to a human body, but not sitting on the lap. No amount of pouncing on pretty kitty and hauling him up to a lap is going to be successful. Even if he wants to sit on a lap, he will jump down from the one he has been plunked onto, wash himself with dignity, and—when he's quite ready—jump up again and make himself comfortable.

Minnie, in all her eighteen years, has never been a lap-sitter. Yet she loves to be close to a warm human, sharing the narrowest seat or crowding close if there is plenty of space. She always waits eagerly, however, for an invitation. Sitting before me with her big green-gold eyes wide and expectant, her feet planted for quick lifting, she waits until

I have patted the seat beside me and invited, "Want to come up, Minnie?"

Little Mr. X, of SuziTu's second litter, before he left me had no such compunctions about protocol and invitations. His first move after having broken fast was to hunt out Madam and her coffee cup, climb up immediately to inspect the coffee, and snuggle down for a little after-dinner nap on my lap. No invitations were needed, no negations heeded. He was one of the few kittens who, from early kittenhood, was a voluntary lap-sitter. Most young cats do not want to rest for a moment except when they fall in their tracks or when their mother corrals them and tucks them away, full of milk and satisfaction.

Whenever I pick up a cat for any reason—seldom without a reason I know the cat will appreciate—I grasp him gently around his middle with one hand extended under his chest, and use the other hand or my hip to support his hind legs. Cats do not like to be dangled, and only a kitten's mother can pick him up correctly and safely by the scruff of the neck. The supporting hand under the hind legs gives cats a feeling of security such as they have when they are on a flat surface, poised for a jump, with all the weight in the rear and the forepaws ready for the next move. I have used this pickup technique successfully even in separating Jo-Jo and SuziTu from the Minnie they had downed—one in each hand, back legs braced against my hip bones. No damage to anyone resulted, except when I grabbed them the wrong way.

People who do not know cats sometimes take fright at a moving tail. I am almost convinced that a cat does not know what his tail is doing. Otherwise, why would kittens be so fascinated with their own? I think they have little conscious control over what their tails do. Yet the tail is a most expressive appendage. Elevated like a flag, it indicates "I'm monarch of all I survey, and I find it good." Dragging dejectedly behind, it means "Nothing is going right today, and I'm expecting the worst to be just around the next corner."

But when a cat is lying down, relaxed as only a cat in repose can be, quite often the very tip of the tail will flap slowly against the floor. This motion, if you listen closely, is usually accompanied by purring. It is a happy gesture. A mother cat willing to play with her kittens, or at least to give them something to chase without bothering much, swishes her tail spasmodically from side to side, inviting the babies to chase it. Only when the tail is attached to an angry-faced, crouching cat and is switching wildly from side to side or thumping up and down is antagonism indicated; except, of course, if the tail fur rises to sausage proportions, to complete the big puffed-up effect of risen fur on the spine, which is the surest indication that the poor cat is terrified and trying to make as big an impression as possible on whatever has frightened him.

Punishment is best meted out in decibels. A cat's ears are exceedingly sensitive, and loud noises—even the unexpected rattling of a paper—scare the stuffings out of him. Did you ever see the terror in a cat's eyes when he hears a loud peal of thunder? Although I have a voice that carries for blocks when I whisper, which is a nuisance when I want to say something confidential in public, I do not normally raise it. But when righteous indignation sets in, I bellow.

Common practice in punishing a cat is to slam a folded newspaper down behind him. The basic theory is to produce a loud and sudden noise. I never slap a cat for punishment. They are so fragile in bone structure that it would be too easy to do serious damage in a fit of anger or in justified correction. And besides, the most effective punishment is to associate the loud noise with the *place* or *thing* that was the object of the cat's attention at the time of the crime. When I want to stop a cat from scratching on a chair, I whack the chair where the scratching was being perpetrated and say "No!" To whack the offending paws could quite possibly injure them. If a human is consistent in the training process, the cat very shortly gets the idea. Nothing is wrong with his paws, but something is wrong with those places where he is using them. Naturally, punishment must follow crime immediately. To punish a cat in the evening for something he did at breakfast time makes no sense to him at all.

I have never had any real disciplinary problems concerning my own treasured possessions. When I have something new that is special and untouchably mine, I point it out, let the cats smell it, explain to them that this is Madam's and we must be very careful of it, and this is what it looks like, how it smells, how it feels. No mystery, no reason for dangerous investigation. At the same time, after they have had a chance to get thoroughly acquainted with the untouchable, I give them something interesting that is distinctly theirs. A new little rubber ball, a catnip mouse, or even the wrappings in which my new treasure was swathed will do. As a result, I still add to my collection of Wedgwood from time to time and keep it all within reach of the cats, who never touch it. It has become part of the rest of the uninteresting-to-cats scenery. We have no problems.

Christmas trees, coming once a year, are naturally of great interest. All those bright, shiny things hanging where a paw can reach out and bat! So I hang a few glittering paper ones on a low branch and let the cats have their fun. I always make a Christmas floral arrangement just for them, knowing that they are going to tear it apart eventually. They dislike the taste or texture of Christmas greens, but they do love to pull them out of the flower holder and play with them. It does no harm and gives them a sense of participation during a season when their people are obviously excited.

In the summer, I make arrangements of fresh flowers for myself that they are not allowed to touch, but may always smell if they wish (and they usually do, because cats frequently love perfumes); and I set a bowl of pansies where they can pull them out, chew on them, and play with them —they belong to them, and they know it.

I have tried to persuade my cats to use a scratching post. Perhaps I have not tried hard enough, for I have been successful only with SuziTu, while the others ignore the post entirely. Anne's cats happily stretch and sharpen their claws on their post a dozen times a day, and I keep hoping SuziTu will set a good example for Minnie and Jo-Jo that eventually will lead them to do likewise.

Once I bought a substantial, bark-covered post with a catnip mouse suspended from a wire spring on top, tall enough for a mature cat's stretching full-length and with a firm base under it. It was just what a cat should want, but neither Minnie nor Monnie would give it more than a passing glance. They went right on scratching on a slip-covered chair back.

"All right," I said. "If you like that slip cover so much, I'll slip-cover the post." I fastened a quilted pad around the post and stitched a neat casing of their favorite slip-cover fabric, left over from my upholstering job. I pulled the casing on and set the post temptingly where Minnie and Monnie could get at it at will. Monnie had watched me prepare it, a supercilious grin on his face, and when it was finished, he gave me an open sneer and walked past the post, skirting it as widely as possible, to scratch deliberately on the chair with its identical but faded covering. Once in a while, Minnie would give the post an absentminded pat, but never as a substitute for the chair. So I gave up. You can lead a cat to the post, I concluded, but you cannot make him scratch it.

The scratching-post conflict remained a thorn in my flesh for years. I considered the cats' refusal to use one as a rather personal denial of all my theories about love conquering all. It seemed to me that the less I said about how easy it is to train cats to use a post, the better off I would be. And people who give me reasons why they cannot have cats in their homes always bring up the subject.

So SuziTu won a special prize from me when visiting friends spotted our newest post, neatly covered with carpeting and adorned with a mobile cat toy. "Of course," said one friend confidently, "cats never use a scratching post." SuziTu, who had apparently been sound asleep on the sofa, rose from it and walked quickly over to the post, where she proceeded without a word or "look-at-me" glance to scratch diligently and long. Then she returned, also without a glance at anyone, to her sofa corner and feigned sleep.

One night I did something inadvertent that taught me another lesson, for I never knowingly torment a cat or make him unhappy without a reason. Occasionally, it is just convenient (when I am serving fish for dinner, for instance) to put a closed door between the cats and me for a while. When I do this unusual thing, it is absolutely necessary to explain to them that they are not being punished. I found that out the hard way when Jo-Jo was a kitten.

I did not want him to bother me while I ate my dinner, so I shut him in the kitchen alone, where his own food was. He set up a noisy hue and cry, which I took to be anger and frustration. But when I had finished my meal and opened the barrier, the poor little cat rubbed frantically against my ankles, trembling and frightened, wanting to be reassured of my approval and affection. His cries had been simple terror, not anger. It was the first (and last) time I ever willfully shut him into a room alone. But sometimes he accidentally shuts himself into the powder room, and I have to extricate him. As he goes around the partly open door toward his box, he may brush against it, making it swing closed. The panic in his voice is truly pathetic, for he suffers from claustrophobia. Of late, I have taken to placing a little door-stopper in both bathroom doorways so that the cats can get in and out of their boxes without problems of this sort. It may baffle my guests a bit when they try to close the doors, but I prefer baffled guests to trapped cats.

10

Togetherness

A most touching example of togetherness came into my view by coincidence last summer. I had stopped at a gas station in a country village to have my car refueled. While I was waiting for my change, another car drove in and pulled up on the opposite side of the pump. A young man alighted and began to remove the crepe-paper streamers that decorated his car, and their removal revealed the "Just Married" announcement that his prankish friends had painted on the sides of the shiningly clean vehicle.

His bride, still wearing her going-away corsage, remained in the car, the back seat of which was filled to overflowing with luggage and gift-wrapped packages. In her hand, she held the end of a long, slender leash, and atop the packages behind her was a magnificent Siamese cat, whose collar was attached to the other end of the leash.

"Was he a wedding present?" I asked.

"No," was all she had time to say, as I received my change and drove off, reflecting on the beauty of a marriage for three.

The question of leaving home sometimes takes a bit of solving. Of course, if people spend the summer in the country, the cat goes along. But if it is a vacation trip or a weekend, it is not always possible to take the cat, and some cats are agonizingly miserable in transit.

Traveling with a cat by car requires about the same precautions as traveling with a small child. You need to take a litter box along, some small cans of cat food and a can opener, a feeding dish, and most important, a long leash attached to a collar around the cat's neck, unless he is confined in a carrying case at all times. On a long motor trip, with overnight stops scheduled, it is important to check in advance with the hotels and motels where you plan to stop, to be sure there is no rule against pets. Most hostelries that refuse to accept dogs will usually be willing to let you keep your housebroken cat with you, but it is best to find out before you make a reservation.

On trains, boats, and planes, you will need a carrying case, and sometimes you will be allowed to keep the cat with you; sometimes he will be banished to the baggage section. Again, check in advance and find out what facilities are available to keep the cat happy, comfortable, and healthy. Especially if you are traveling overseas to land at a foreign port, be sure to find out what regulations of quarantine, shots, and such are applicable. They vary from country to country, and unless you plan to relocate permanently abroad, it may be better to leave the cat at home.

Some cats love to ride in cars. Alice, for example, went

to the country happily, whether for the weekend or the entire summer. She loved the freedom of roaming over a grassy lawn and willingly climbed into her traveling case when she was told "it's time to go to the country." (She was less eager to return to her city apartment, but remained a good traveler in the car.)

Domino, unlike Alice, used to spend the eight hours of his trips from Buffalo to Connecticut crouched wretchedly on the floor of the car, illness written all over his poor little face.

To Minnie and Monnie, the carrying case invariably meant a trip to Dr. Roth, and gentle as he is with cats, their visits to his office were seldom associated with real pleasure. It was absolutely impossible to persuade them that a trip in a carrying case was going to be fun, nor could I have enjoyed their yowling protesting company. So whenever I was to be away for more than a couple of days, I had to arrange for cat-sitters. My friends were usually quite readily available, and although the cats were flatteringly a bit lonely for my company and always glad to have me return, I knew they were well cared for. I always left a care-and-feeding schedule posted where my sitters could easily find it. It detailed the whereabouts of the cat food and litter, the amounts and procedures for feeding each day, instructions for taking care of the litter box, and prominently, Dr. Roth's phone number in case of trouble.

When I went to Europe for seven weeks, however, I had to make long-term arrangements, of course. I left Minnie, Suzanne, and Josephus at home, and Elsie agreeably changed her once-a-week schedule to an hour-a-day visit, during which she fed them, took care of their box, and played with them. Playing was important, because human companionship is as much a necessity as food and water for possessing cats. They fared very well during my absence, since Elsie shares my love of felines. After that time, as long as I lived in the city, it was standard practice for Elsie to cat-sit with "her babies" whenever I was away for more than a weekend.

The first time I moved from one apartment to another with cats was a traumatic experience for Monnie and Minnie. They howled from their carrying cases throughout the short cab ride across town, while the cab driver gleefully reported on cats who, miles from their former homes, had spent months trudging back to their original headquarters. Released from their cases, both Monnie and Minnie made for the farthest corner of the stall shower, as though they had studied the floor plan of the new apartment and knew exactly where best to hide. There they stayed throughout the day and first night, while the movers brought in familiar furniture, dumped it in the center of the unfamiliar rooms, and left it to me to place it where I wanted it. From time to time, I responded to the pitiful wails that emanated spasmodically from the stall shower, but nothing would persuade the cats to come out and explore their new home until, exhausted, I fell into bed.

Sometime during the night they must have done their investigating, recognized the familiar-smelling chairs and sofa, and discovered that beyond the open door of my new bedroom, I was asleep in the bed they knew so well. For the next morning, come breakfast time, the tails were hoisted like flags as they paced the length of the hall, unerringly steering me through the still-wrecked-looking living room, and parked themselves expectantly in front of the kitchen sink. All was well with their new world, and tails never expressed more pleasurable excitement. The new world was so much bigger for exploration!

The second move was a bit easier, but attracted more attention from the public. We moved from one building to another in the same housing development, a distance of approximately a city block. Josephus and Suzanne presented no problems. They settled down together in a carrying case and had a nap while they awaited transportation. But Minnie had taken refuge from confusion by mounting to the top of the broom closet, and with all the furniture gone, I had no way of reaching her. Cajoling brought no results, but for once nature and force of habit worked for me. Minnie had to come down to use the litter box, and once down, found nowhere to hide.

With difficulty, I caught her, stuffed her into a neighbor's carrying case hastily borrowed for the occasion, and prepared to set forth. I had the frame of my grandson's folding baby carriage, which made a wonderful double-decker delivery cart, with one case on the top deck, the other on the bottom, and the litter box and feeding dishes tucked in beside them.

This was efficient transportation during our brief walk, for New Yorkers are accustomed to seeing unusual carts being pushed along the city streets. But this one was vocal. Before the elevator had reached the basement level, Minnie's anguished yowlings had wakened and disturbed Suzanne and Josephus, who raised their voices in wild alarm, Suzanne outdoing herself in Siamese screeches. Trying to soothe them, I outshouted them all—in my most beseeching Siamese tones—and thus we proceeded along the wide street that borders one of New York's "exclusive, quiet residential developments." I decided that it was better not to move again.

Whenever I have sold a kitten, one question constantly

recurred: What kind of bed shall I fix for him? I cannot conceive of a cat-loving human not wanting to share his own bed with the cat who loves him, but some cats prefer not to sleep with people, despite the feline love of body warmth. The bedding question has never been a problem for me, because my cats have always enjoyed sleeping wherever I slept, each cat having a preferred place.

Minnie likes to take over the other pillow on my bed, close to my face. Whichever side I turn to in my restless sleep, she moves herself so that she faces me. Monnie used to like to lie across my ankles; and Suzanne preferred a middle-of-the-road position. Some of my cats have enjoyed sleeping under the covers, which was Monnie's preference in wintertime; but Minnie apparently shares Jo-Jo's claustrophobia to some extent and never took to the undercover position unless her head was on a pillow, nose uncovered.

The first night Suzanne and Joey spent with us, I had to leave them in the living room so Minnie would have an opportunity to adjust to their presence in her house. Next morning I found them rolled up together like a little black-and-white ball atop the back of the sofa. It was not long, however, before they moved their nighttime headquarters to my bed, with Minnie's approval, and I must say there were times when I found their presence a little trying. They woke with the first crack of dawn and merrily set upon each other like a couple of little gladiators, leaping over my recumbent form, pouncing on me, rolling over and over around and above me in a consistently successful effort to rouse me. As soon as I showed signs of relatively open eyes (an optical illusion), they began to lick my face, nibble my ears and hair, pat my cheeks, crawl under the covers and out again—you name it, they did it. So in self-defense, I got up. Who wouldn't?

Alice was one of the few cats I know who appeared to enjoy sleeping in her own basket bed. It had a comfortable cushion, was easy for her to climb into, had a protectively raised back to keep off drafts, and was placed in a warm corner of the kitchen where she could retire happily when people got to be too much for her.

Other cats I have known, of those who either preferred not to sleep with people or were not allowed to do so, usually have chosen for themselves a favorite chair, a cushion, a pile of clean dusting cloths—something warm, soft, and protected in its location. Absolutely nothing could change their determination to sleep there. Once a cat's mind is made up, not even an act of Congress can change it.

The basic interrelationship between humans and cats need not be complicated at all. Humans complicate it when they fail to recognize that, above all, a cat must maintain his dignity, must feel that he is receiving due respect, and must be allowed to make his own decisions at his own time. Consider for a moment the enormous difference between your size and the cat's and give honor to his courage in making his personality felt so strongly.

Cats know exactly what their value is. Money being meaningless to them, "value" is whatever is available to give or to receive. So a cat who decides to live with a poor man who honestly loves him never complains about the absence of chicken livers for breakfast. He does with what his possessed has to offer and adds to his diet as necessary by foraging. If his possessed human loves him dearly, the cat will share willingly after he has provided for himself and is naturally disappointed if his human seems not to appreciate a nice fresh-caught mouse or fish head brought in as a thank-you.

Indoor cats who never go outdoors at all, I have discovered, will happily take over the management of your home, putting it onto a workable cat-oriented schedule. They will baby-sit diligently and carefully; scare the living daylights out of intruders; graciously entertain you and your properly introduced friends of whom they approve; expect a bare minimum of extra housekeeping from you; understand your problems and offer sage advice; and love, love, love you when you want their expressed affection. There is one prerogative on which they firmly insist: If they decide to use the furniture as a scratching post, it must be clearly understood that this is what they are going to do unless you change their minds. In all other respects, cats will graciously agree to human preferences whenever these preferences are convenient for the cats and make sense to them.

Naturally, the indoor cat will probably want to make a few alterations here and there in the personalities and habits of his humans. These alterations, of course, are always improvements, such as making a sluggard into an early riser.

Outdoor cats will gladly give you similar companionship when they have time and opportunity. But outdoor cats have work to do, keeping mice out of the barn, patrolling the surrounding lawns and driveways, and checking into the intentions of people who approach the house. These tasks tend to limit the cat's time for being companionable and to color his attitude toward play. If an outdoor cat has an open invitation to come into the house whenever he feels like it or to spend the night indoors as he should certainly be allowed to do, he will have much more time and inclination for giving freely of his companionship and understanding.

If he is really happy, from time to time he may invite his friends for dinner and allow his humans to treat them as cordially as they treat their own friends. In exchange, if his friends enjoy the hospitality, they may be willing to stay and even raise families for you.

In either case, indoor cats or outdoor cats will give friendship, love, respect, and understanding to humans in the exact degree that they receive the same benefits from those humans. No more, no less. You gets what you gives. A cat's friendship can be a beautiful thing, as any cat-lover knows; but, of course, you have to earn it. Putting food in a dish is nowhere near enough. A human must really care about a cat if he wants the cat to give more than two hmm-mm's about him.

I do not mean that, once acquainted, Mr. Cat should be allowed to have his own way invariably. The rules must be made and enforced. But he will want to learn the rules to please his humans, after he is sure they are really his humans.

Mowser, for instance, knows that it irritates his people when they have to open doors for him. Since he lives a good bit of the time in the sweet-smelling wilderness that surrounds his home, he frequently wants out. It has become his custom, therefore, to open any doors that are insecurely latched and quietly take his departure, leaving the door open to the extent of space needed for him to pass through—and he is a fairly wide cat. His people complain that he does not close the doors after himself, which I am convinced he could have been taught to do earlier in his life. Like Monster, he is an unusually intelligent, very cooperative cat—with the people he loves. In return, he is a highly respected member of his family.

Last year, Mowser ran up his family's doctor bills more than anyone else. His troubles stemmed from a misconception, formed early in his life, of just how big and formidable he is.

Way back in his youth, shortly after he had chosen his

family, Mowser stepped off his terrace with arched back and a frightening hiss aimed at a neighbor's poodle, who was busily tearing freshly laundered sheets off the clothesline in Mowser's backyard. Mowser's menace happened to coincide with his human's reaction to being fed up with this repeated performance from the trespassing dog. As Mowser advanced on his prey, his human fired a blast of salt pellets at the offending dog's rear. The dog went off fundamentally unharmed, but stung and yipping noisily. Mowser sat down and washed himself proudly, convinced that he had vanquished the enemy with his ferocious warning.

During the ensuing years, when Mowser and his family had moved to a new neighborhood, passing dogs quickly learned to give wide berth to the black cat who walked fearlessly toward them with fire in his eye and sharp claws on his toes. With the unspoken communication system working well, dogs have had no doubt as to Mowser's territorial claims, or what would happen to them if they encroached upon them.

The wild life, however, proved to be a different matter. A muskrat lives in the pond. A huge woodchuck has a home somewhere in an adjoining field. A raccoon occasionally investigates the garbage cans. There are countless long-toothed rabbits, in addition to inoffensive smaller creatures. Last summer, Mowser came home in sad condition. The first time, someone had taken a large bite out of his hip. It became infected, and when first aid failed to relieve it, he had to go to the hospital. The wound was exceedingly deep—straight through to the bone—and gangrene was just around the corner.

Somewhat diminished in his self-evaluation, Mowser was fairly cautious about going out at night after his recovery. But one of his wild acquaintances apparently tangled with him in broad daylight. When he had been missing too long, Barbara finally located him in a thicket of the woods, quietly waiting for the end. She picked him up tenderly and brought him home to her hospital-trained mother. This time, it was his eye that had been damaged. It was swollen shut, and on close examination, tooth marks were plainly visible in the injured eyelid. Again his vet effected a cure, and now Mowser is more careful than ever, keeping to the open spaces when he cruises down the lawn toward the pond, knowing that there is a good reason why he is not allowed to go out at night, even if the moon is bright and full. Perhaps he has learned his lesson, and in his elderly fashion, decided that wisdom is the better part of valor. At least, he is cooperative about the restrictions placed on his prowling.

Mowser's attitude toward other creatures brings up another question that is frequently asked of me: "I have a dog —or a canary—or goldfish. What will happen if I bring a cat into my home?"

It is a good question, and people experienced with cats will answer cagily, "Well, it all depends . . ." and hope they will not be asked to elaborate. Who can tell what or whom any individual, cat or human, will consider bosom-pal material or a hated enemy?

Yet just as children recognize no barriers of race, creed, color, or formation in other children, young animals with four feet can trustfully be said, in generalization, to grow up together in complete happiness if they start out together.

Kittens and puppies under six months old when they are introduced seem to see no reason why they should not get along. After that, it's chancy, mostly because the cat is so individualistic. Dogs, I think, are more malleable, more willing to live happily with cats; but they are afraid, with good reason, of a cat's fighting tactics and equipment. When a cat fights a larger, more earth-bound animal, he lights on the back of the enemy and reaches, claws out, for its eyes. Most dogs are larger than most cats. Most dogs who tangle physically with cats in battle end up suffering major or minor injuries. And the alleged intuitive distrust between cats and dogs seems to be more pronounced in teen-age and mature animals than in babies. Anne's Marmalade II was about eight months old when I watched him chase a playful half-grown dog out of his yard while Valentina watched from her hastily arranged perch in a tree.

To add a cat to a dog-loving family takes two ingredients: The people themselves must understand the vastly different characteristics and personality traits of cats and dogs, must love and understand both equally; and must be constantly vigilant until the cat-and-dog relationship has firmed up on a mutual-friendship basis. It happens successfully. Usually, it happens with an opposite-sex combination—a female cat who will probably rather quickly convince a male dog that Miss Cat is boss; or the other way 'round—a motherly bitch who is willing to take a young male kitten under her maternal wing.

The "intuitive-hatred" theory is a hard one. No one can deny that instinctive traits exist in all our little quadruped friends. Nor can anyone who knows cats at all deny that fish and fowl are favorite foods. Tropical fish present an easy problem to solve if you have a cat living with you. Most cats are aware that a tiny fish will not provide them their daily allotment of food, but it *moves*. So it should be fun to put a paw into the aquarium and catch this moving object. Caught, of course, it proves edible, but the average cat who dips into the aquarium is merely playing. A screen to cover the top of the goldfish bowl will keep your fish safe.

Birds are something else again. In all my research, I have found nothing but freak situations in which pet birds and house-bound cats, given freedom of contact, do not end up in a house-bound cat and an empty cage. If you have pet birds and cats in the same household and like the birds, I would suggest that you keep the birds caged at all times with a firm, cat-proof latch on the cage door.

11

Fun and Games

People who want a pet animal to stand up and beg, to turn somersaults on command, to follow to heel, to jump through hoops, can train an intelligent, willing, loving cat to do all those things. But such tricks are not catly. The cat who allows them to be foisted on him is not a normal, secure cat, unless he thought up the program himself. If *he* initiates the game, and you praise him for it and help him to perfect it, he is having a wonderful time. He will do his tricks whenever he feels like it, never just because you command him to show off. If you want a constantly delightful, unpredictable companion with a mind of his own, let a cat possess you.

Anyone who has ever watched a pair of kittens sitting on an air conditioner, literally batting the breeze with their tiny paws, or seen a cat trying to catch the ball in a baseball game or golf match on television, knows that few cat toys are necessary. Cats make up their own games; either ask their people to participate or play with each other; and usually prefer to initiate their own sports.

Of course, a catnip mouse is endless fun (until the scent wears out or the mouse is chewed to shreds) for a mature cat. Kittens do not seem to be interested in this stimulant and certainly do not need it, but it makes an adult cat act like a kitten. Because I read that catnip is an irritant to kidney-troubled cats (which Dr. Roth says is untrue), I have had few catnip toys around until recently, lest they revive Minnie's cystitis.

Little rubber jack balls have always been standard equipment for my cat family. They are small enough to fit into a cat's mouth, large enough not to be swallowed. They roll easily. They have nothing cat-harmful inside them. They are soft enough so that if I step on one, it will not throw me. The only problem I have had with them is that they disappeared behind the apartment refrigerator and none of us could ever retrieve them from there.

I make a careful distinction between our favorite jack balls and the more expensive golf balls. For one reason, golf balls are hard and could hurt my feet or throw me. But if a golf ball is opened up, as old ones sometimes are, it contains yards and yards of elastic banding. If a cat should swallow any large quantity of this thin rubber stripping, it could be even more dangerous than swallowed string. True, it might chance to pass through the intestines and be eliminated. But the chances are at least fifty–fifty that it could instead wind itself around the intestines, causing intestinal strangulation.

There is a theory that sponge-rubber balls are dangerous to cats if the animals chew them, because the sponge rubber could adhere to the intestines and clog them. In my own experience with many cats and numerous balls, I feel quite secure in saying that it would take a much larger animal with much longer teeth to chew a sponge-rubber ball into pieces small enough to swallow. Our jack balls are pock-marked with tiny indentations from cat teeth, but they have never been bitten into pieces, nor even lost little chunks from the surfaces.

So I have bought a succession of these useful little balls over the years. Some come with jacks, some with a long rubber string attached to a paddle (and I detach the ball from the string). Some are just the way they all end up—with nothing added. They provide continuous enjoyment for cats of all ages, although I have noticed that kittens sometimes prefer to bat and chase a somewhat larger ball of soft rubber, about the size of a baseball, perhaps because they see it as something tremendous and challengingly important to tackle. Kittens are notoriously playful, but usually prefer to play with each other or with their parents rather than with people, until they are about two months old, except when there is only one of the litter left.

Empty spools are fun for them, and they have no compunction about playing with spools that are not empty, tangling the thread or yarn hopelessly. Thread can be dangerous, though, if they eat it.

Empty paper bags were made especially for kittens to hide in, so that a littermate or a parent can jump on it, roll it over and over, and pretend not to know that it is occupied. A cardboard carton is a real bonanza, especially if it is complete with flaps. A kitten can jump onto the unsealed top flaps, plunge inside, and pose cutely with his little head poked out before he re-emerges.

Buttons are as good as balls, but have to be large enough so that they cannot be swallowed. If they're attached to something that a human is wearing at the moment, they are that much more fun, because the human is usually opposed to having them chewed off. And the standard toy for young and not-so-young cats is a piece of fabric or a strip of cardboard tied to the end of a long string.

SuziTu played actively with her kittens as they grew up. When they were a month old, they began to be real clowns: fearlessly climbing (and falling from three-foot heights), batting SuziTu's slowly waving tail as she allowed a hungry one to continue nursing, and endlessly teasing each other. One would gallop up behind a brother, grab brother's leg, and pull it out from under so that they fell in a heap together, pretending to fight to the death. They would stand up on their hind legs like squirrels eating nuts, batting each other with their forepaws. And suddenly, they would all lie down in their tracks, exhausted.

My tall, woven-hemp scrap basket was just made for kittens. I kept it partly under a small stand because it fitted there closely enough so that it would not tip over and spoil their fun when the kittens climbed it. It was a safety home, a hiding place, a secluded bed, a mountain to climb, a two-foot drop to jump into, a scratching post.

The floor-to-ceiling draperies provided hours of fun for them, too. Experienced as I am in sharing a home with cats and kittens, I had made my drapes of sturdy, closely woven cotton fabric—no danger of little claws getting caught in pulled threads. At times, all four kittens were actively progressing up or down the drapes at the same time. Typically, if one started a game, the others joined in immediately, for there were no rugged individualists in the second litter, as Jennie was in the first. (Jennie was always preoccupied with something on her own—waking up to the game or the availability of a meal several minutes after everyone else was deeply involved.)

When they began to play with me, the kittens seemed charmed by my imitating their gleeful piping "wee-yew." All I had to do by the time they were a month old, when SuziTu began to allow them a little more freedom, was pipe "wee-yew, wee-yew" and four tiny balls of fur would prance out of their home cloister to greet me. By then they liked to have me roll a ball across the floor—not too fast, just gently. And of course, a wad of paper on the end of a swinging string was "such fun, Madam."

I tried to avoid getting them overtired. Once, when there was only one of the litter left with us, I had a guest who loved kittens and tirelessly swung the paper wad on its string for the kitten to chase. The little cat ran, ran, ran very fast. The paper kept swinging. He ran, ran, ran a little slower. The paper kept swinging. He ran—and he ran—and—he—r-a-n. Finally, he simply could not stand up any longer, even though the paper kept swinging. It is difficult to tell a sensitive cat-lover that she is overdoing the play, that the kitten is too tired to play, and should be allowed to rest. The kitten told her himself.

Hide-and-seek is a game that every kitten I have known loves to initiate either with other cats or with people. Part of the success of the project, of course, is to take the victim by surprise, and part of the human's share in the game is to pretend to be surprised, even when he knows the assault is coming. This is guaranteed to make a kitten's little face open up into a pink triangle of laughter.

There was one weekend when, as I took off for the country, I failed to locate Monster. He loved to play hide-and-seek with me, and although he heard me call him, it was his idea of real sport not to answer. This time, I could not stop to play games with him. I was catching a train, and I knew he was somewhere about. Remembering the day he had spent zipped up in a garment bag as a result of playing this game, I pulled down all the zippers, found no sign of him, and went off, confident that he would come out of hiding when he realized I was gone.

When I returned from my weekend, there was no Monster to greet me at the door. I called, and searching the apartment, finally heard a faint response. "Monnie, where *are* you?" I asked. Again a faint voice answered from the bedroom, and I opened a little-used closet. Monster had spent the entire weekend shut up in that closet without food or water.

This time, the game had not turned out to be all fun. There were blue rings under his eyes, and his white face looked drawn. He came out rubbing against my ankles, apologetic and crestfallen. Checking the closet, I found the reason for his apology. In dire urgency, he had carefully torn a plastic covering off an evening gown, spread it on the closet floor, and made a small puddle in the middle of it. Monster would rather pop a gusset than piddle in the wrong place, but in the course of two days, he had had no choice. After that, I never left the house without either knowing exactly where all the cats were or leaving every door ajar.

SuziTu, when free of the responsibilities of motherhood, is a gay little girl, full of playful antics. One of her favorite tricks is to stand behind me and suddenly jump, landing on my back at about waist level. She weighs all of four pounds and is as light on her paws as a dancer. When I feel the tiny pressure behind me, it is my cue to reach around and support her gently under her rear end. (This has the double advantage of removing her claws from my flesh.) Then it is her move, and she circles around my waist until she can turn her purring, laughing little face up to mine, saying "Ye-oow" happily, continue on up to my shoulder, and decide whether she will ride a while or jump down so that we can do it all over again.

This is great sport when I am wearing enough clothes. She weighs so little and uses her claws so slightly that she has never torn a shred of fabric I was wearing; but skin is another matter, and we had to establish a rigid rule about this game at the outset. It was fortunate that shortly after SuziTu initiated this gleeful assault I was standing before a mirror, searching for underpinnings in my dresser drawer. I saw her crouch, prepared to spring, and issued a very firm negative bellow. "Wait, Suzi! You'll hurt Madam!"

SuziTu understood and cooperated. She restrained herself until I had donned some protective coverings, sitting patiently behind me, her blue eyes alight with anticipation. "O.K., Suzi," I said. "Now it's all right." Then happily she jumped. Once in a while she catches herself about to jump before I am dressed, remembers, and waits. She learned quickly and obeys the rules because I do let her have her fun, the only restriction being a reasonable regard for my own skin.

Unlike Monnie, Jo-Jo loves his mirror game. There are several large mirrors hung where, when he stands level with them, he can reach up for a view of an entire room. He especially enjoys the one in the bedroom, because there he finds my reflection late at night or early in the morning and I wave at him from my bed. So far, he has never waved back, probably because his bright smile is enough response or because he is in need of both forepaws to keep from falling from his perch.

Closets seem to have a special fascination for most cats. Minnie used to like to sit squarely in the shadows on the floor of my unlighted closet and disappear completely, merely by shutting her eyes. Her black coat blended perfectly with the shadows, and she knew I could not see her, so we played hide-and-seek the lazy way.

SuziTu and Jo-Jo seized every opportunity to occupy a shelf in the apartment linen closet for a peaceful little interlude or busy investigation. And time and again, I have had to crawl among boxes in the storage closet to find a peeping kitten who, exploring, thought he was lost.

The bedroom has its own attractions. There are so many things a cat can do there to stir up fun and frolic and to get the day's activities under way. Bedrooms have dresser drawers that, when open, are wonderful for exploration. First, of course, the searching paw must displace everything in the drawer to expose what is underneath. Then the resulting confusion of soft clothing makes a wonderful nest in which to settle down for a nap, or just for wakeful observation. I have often told Minnie she belonged in a department store, in ladies' underwear. That is her favorite drawer.

Some bedrooms, like the one in which Alice's people sleep, have tall dressers that provide adequate advantages in themselves. Alice liked to mount the dresser so that she could jump down upon a sleeping human, arriving on an unsuspecting body with a satisfying "plunk." This technique was sure to elicit response when she had failed to rouse the sleeper by hurling books to the floor.

My own bookcase headboard offers numerous delights that can be used for blackmail, too. There is the box of tissues, for one. A mess of torn-up tissues is certain to bring reaction from me, because they clog the vacuum cleaner and consequently have to be picked up by hand. And books can easily be pushed off onto my weary head, which is one sure way of getting breakfast. Long ago, I removed to a safer place the little replica of a witch's iron pot.

Of course, hitting me on the head is a last resort, perhaps

because other methods of waking me do not bring forth such wrathful response. There is the kissing method; a cool, wet little nose nuzzling my cheek makes me wake up smiling. There's the patting method, useful also for getting petted in return. A soft paw with no claws (at first) patting my cheek or forehead usually brings a listless hand out from under the blanket to return the caress. And there is the vocal method—the strident, pitiful, demanding, or put-upon voice in the ear—complaining of neglect, imminent starvation, infinite patience that has reached its end, and outright threats of violence—unless!

Mowser, now that Barbara is married and has moved to her own home, looks to her brother Harold, when he is available, for morning attention. When Mowser deems it time for the day to begin, he storms Harold's bedroom, shouting "Har*row!* Har*row!*" If the door is ajar, and he gets no immediate response, he stands on Harold's chest, shouting in the poor boy's ear until his mission is successful. Harold's freshman year at college must have been hard on Mowser!

Certainly, cats are teasers, but humans should not overdo *their* teasing in return. I have never known a cat to continue to tease after he had achieved what he wanted or beyond the point of endurance when his human prey has sternly ordered a stop. Teasing is fun to a cat only if the teasee does not get angry about it.

So it is when the roles are reversed. A cat may enjoy a bit of teasing up to a point, but at that point should no longer be teased. Not only is there a possibility of sharp-clawed retaliation, well-earned, but there is a more important danger to the cat's overall view of humans. Monster, you will remember, would never have felt so antagonistic toward my guests if two of them had teased him less when he was a tiny kitten.

Purring is a happy indication, and I am always a little sad that I cannot usually hear it in a mature cat. Kittens purr loudly. At nursing time, they produce a good imitation of the sound of a running motor. But when the mature cat purrs, you usually have to feel the vibration in his throat to know it. Only very elderly cats, like Minnie, when they reach second-kittenhood, purr loudly again.

One other real indication of pleasure that is sometimes misunderstood is the cat's habit of extending and retracting his claws. When a cat is relaxed and happy (sometimes purring), it is not at all uncommon for him to lie with his forepaws outstretched, pads up, and work his claws in and out in the air. I think this gesture, too, is beyond the cat's conscious control and is reminiscent of his nursing days. Kittens, busy filling their little bellies from their mother's milk bar, usually stretch their forepaws out on each side of their faces, possibly to stake out their individual territories. The claws work in and out, in and out, until I wonder that their mother has any fur left on her stomach.

Kneading is a gesture of supreme happiness, and I especially welcome it when, as Minnie often does now, the paws are gently placed against my cheek. I feel the tiny nick of claws from time to time, but never a scratch results because no thrust into the skin is intended. It is just another thank-you from a contented, loving cat.

On those occasions when claws do get caught—in skin or fabric—because they have not been trimmed lately and the cat feels insecure, all you have to do to release them without tearing is to press gently on the paw pad. This slight pressure pushes the claw farther out, releasing the catch.

One of the pleasures that my cats have enjoyed during their years with me is music. The most interesting thing about their music appreciation is their variety in tastes. Some like one kind of music, some another.

Monster invariably jumped up onto my lap for a snuggle when I began to play the deep chords that open the Grieg Concerto in A Minor. And when I practiced my favorite Beethoven Sonata, he went into ecstasies over some of the thunderously melodic, stormy passages. On the other hand, he also seemed to enjoy that long rippling run in Paderewski's Minuet in G, which is so entirely different.

Minnie sat impassive during all the concerts Monster and I shared so happily, whether from the piano, the radio, or the phonograph. I concluded that she had no ear for music at all. Then came the Calypso craze, and my mother came back from a trip to Jamaica with every Harry Bellafonte record she could find for me, plus a good collection of steel-drum recordings. As Monnie loved classical piano, so did Minnie love Calypso. She sat before the phonograph enraptured, occasionally uttering a pleased little yelp of response or participation, always keeping her eyes glued to the source of this delight.

Most other vocal music seems to make no impression whatever, except for one record in my collection. I have an old recording by Villa-lobos, in which there are some incredibly high, limpid tones of soprano vocalization, like some weird jungle bird. This is the only vocal music to which my cats have responded (except for Bellafonte), and if I remember correctly, it was Monnie who registered the most interest.

All my cats have shown great enjoyment of whistling. Even though they hate to feel a breeze ruffle their whiskers, they climb inquiringly onto the whistler's chest to get close to the puckered lips that emit the sound. Their reaction to whistling is one of great excitement, somewhat like their frenzy when they hear a fly buzzing.

Kittens, preoccupied with kittenhood, seem impervious to any musical sounds that do not imitate their own or their parents' voices. SuziTu's son, Mr. X, and his pal, Sabrina, showed a marked interest in their owner's hi-fi, but their concentration was on the dangerous project of gnawing through the wires while Harry was away or on jumping onto the moving turntable. Naturally, this did not meet with Harry's encouragement. The kittens could electrocute themselves while they disconnected a valuable instrument; and they could harm the records as well as themselves on the turntable merry-go-round. All I was able to offer Harry in this matter was sympathy, for I have never discovered a foolproof method of preventing kittens from chewing electric wires except to train them out of it with watchful prevention techniques.

I might add, full of virtue and self-satisfaction, that it was Sabrina, not Mr. X, who instigated all the various troubles those two caused for Harry. On the other hand, I have to admit that Mr. X was never one to lag behind when someone of his litter said "Let's. . . ." The only difference seems to be that he does not think of the deviltry first. Perhaps he was being polite to Sabrina, who had lived with Harry a few weeks longer and was therefore the established boss of the household.

Undoubtedly, Monster was a superintelligent cat. He was also enough of a politician to do the popular thing if it was going to get him what he wanted. So he never gave me the blank stare of "I don't understand" when, after he had made it clear that he expected some of my dinner, I promised, "Yes, Monnie. I'll give you some when I'm finished with it. But for now, you will please *sit down and wait.*"

Monster sat down and waited. He said nothing during the waiting period, but his eyes never left what he was after. Without turning his head, he could follow every move of my fork from plate to mouth and back to plate again. "I'm not rushing you, of course—but I expect to be served without too much horsing around," his eyes said. At times, he was a bit annoying, like a dinner guest who keeps looking at his wrist watch while dinner is still in progress. But it developed into such a firm habit that eventually, when I was feasting on something Monster wanted, he just came to sit down and wait expectantly beside my chair, without even the suggestion of a promise from me.

If perchance I was dining on something I could not share with him, I immediately explained it to him, told him why, and said I was sorry. Sometimes he did not believe me until he had patiently waited for an empty plate, sniffed it to make sure I was not kidding, and given me a baleful look. "Sit down and wait" was a command that he obeyed under any and all circumstances, because it always meant that something he wanted would be forthcoming.

"Bring it to Madam" is another stock phrase that both Monster and SuziTu found fun and meaningful, since it was derived from the retrieving game. (SuziTu also retrieves, as many Siamese do, and gave her kittens a few preliminary lessons in the art before she dismissed them from her school.) Sometimes this phrase works with other objects that are not too large to be carried, but usually it is a jack ball.

A few months after Monster came to live with us, I began working at home. He loved having me available all day long, and we had to throttle the problem of his interfering with my work schedule. He was cooperative, but he discovered that there was one interruption that was sure to capture me: When he really wanted my attention, he searched the house until he found a little jack ball, picked it up in his teeth, carried it to a point two inches from my feet, and dropped it there. If he accidentally dropped it farther away, he either picked it up again or rolled it with excellent putting strokes to the desired spot. Then, looking up, he spoke—a special little sound that he never used for anything else—demanding that I throw the ball so he could retrieve it.

This was a trick that I found irresistible, and since he was reasonable about it, letting me get back to work after a few minutes of play, I seldom let him down when he started the game. When I could not afford any more time, I told him so, and after a try or two, he would quietly go somewhere else and leave me to my task.

Sometimes, I started the game. "Monster! Where's the ball?" And Monnie went immediately to where he thought he had seen it last, or searched the corners, peered under the furniture, or dove into closets. Sometimes we both peered together, side by side on the floor, until we found it. If it was not wedged in an inaccessible spot, he would get it out and bring it to me. If it was out of his reach, he would dance around talking about it until I moved away whatever obstacle prevented his retrieving it, and we were off in a gay game.

He brought the ball to me several times a day, and more often at night, when I was away from my desk. But only once after Minnie retrieved to his satisfaction, perhaps five years later, did he express any urge to play ball again. That was a time when he caught me napping.

Suddenly, without any preamble, he uttered the special little cry that had always been his signal for ball-playing. And I had forgotten its meaning. Several times he spoke and finally spelled it out for me by peering into corners, reaching with a hooking paw into shadows, until I remembered, apologized, and found the ball for him. Perhaps my slowness at that time discouraged him. He probably thought I was getting too old to play the game. It was the last time he ever mentioned ball-playing.

People sometimes say a cat is a vain creature. I prefer to think that beautiful animals know they are beautiful, expect to be admired, and enjoy it when their beauty is recognized. What is wrong with admitting something that is obviously true? Only *people* have that peculiar concept that, in the face of a well-earned compliment, they should modestly deny it has any possible basis in truth.

"Pretty kitty," consequently, has always been the magic phrase in my family. It makes a cat smile. It did more than that to Monster. It made him lie down and roll over onto his back, paws crossed on his chest, posing until I had satisfied his ego. It took me a while to catch on, but he was a patient teacher. When he lay down on his back, crossed his paws over his chest, and grinned at me, he looked especially appealing. So naturally, I said, "Pretty kitty, Monnie." It came to be a habit in which he indulged whenever he wanted attention and praise. I learned the trick, and if I was too distracted or busy to participate when he asked for it, he would lie there until I did my part, even if it took me a half hour to settle down to the job of paying him his just due.

I do not know what there is about a camera that automatically tells a cat "this is going to make history of your beauty," but every cat I have known has liked to have his picture taken. They never need to be told to "look at the birdie." They are ready at the drop of a flash bulb to hold a stately pose, self-chosen, with rigid attention and pleasant, camera-oriented faces. They will do it as long as the flash bulbs hold out and continue hopefully to find new postures that might be photogenic until I put the camera away. Perhaps this is why there are so many delightful books containing beautiful photographs of cats.

Cats also sit still willingly for my quick pencil sketches, but since sketches take a little longer than a photo, the subjects are likely to become too restive for detailed portraits. Yet I have often thought I detected a wickedly playful glint in an eye as, pencil poised over paper, I was about to capture an attitude that pleased me—only to have my model stretch luxuriously, yawn, and lie down in an entirely different position. "Let's not take so long about this business. How about this pose? Is my best profile showing now?"

Bless their little pointed faces and their big, loyal, loving hearts. If a cat did not put a firm paw down now and then, how could his human remain possessed?

12

The New Life

When it was finally decided that my love affair with a little red house in the country was going to turn into a marriage, I began to worry about how the cats would react to living there. I realized that, although both Jo-Jo and SuziTu had been born in my home town, to which we were returning, they would have no memory of it. They had never been outdoors before I invited them to live with me in the city, and certainly not after. But Minnie was my biggest worry, beginning with the basic question of how in the world I was going to get her into a carrying case on moving day.

Assuming that I might have to resort to a veterinarian-prescribed dosage of aspirin to persuade the old lady into a sleep-dazed trip, where would she want to take up residence? My little house has five rooms, two of which are on the second floor, and I had visions of having to stagger up the stairs each morning with Minnie's breakfast tray, because I knew she would want to sleep with me as always. Well, these things would take care of themselves, I decided, but I spent many a sleepless night trying to persuade myself they would. I would have to play it by ear, but in the meantime, I should start preparing everybody for the move.

One of the interesting things about cats is their response to their people's moods. I was genuinely happy about moving out of the city, and although I told them about it in audible, sales-pitched words, I know it was my brimming-over happy anticipation that made the biggest impression. Jo-Jo and SuziTu smiled at me with their shining blue eyes. They purred and rubbed against my legs. They teased each other like kittens and played tag through the apartment. "When are we going? Let's get this move under way. We'll help you pack!"

I spent more time discussing it with Minnie, stroking her sleek black coat and assuring her that she was going to be with me always, that she would like the country. (I was less convinced about the latter than I sounded.) She smiled reassuringly, nuzzled her head in my hand, and purred loudly, but I was not at all certain she knew what I was talking about. She just knew that I was happy, and that made her happy, too—for the moment, I told myself pessimistically.

When Jo-Jo and SuziTu said they would help me pack, they meant it. They went at the job with a vengeance, jumping into cartons just as I was trying to get some carefully wrapped breakables into a safe corner; chasing the ends of my ropes (sometimes figurative rope ends, too) as I tied a finished box; and running out to the incinerator with me every time I took another load of dispensables.

They were as excited as though it were Christmas, and although they slowed me down in my work, I was glad they were not cowering in fright and howling from a dark corner. I would have disintegrated completely.

In the midst of my second and final week of packing, SuziTu came into heat and demanded frequent petting and cajoling, but her general attitude was a bit tongue-in-cheek. "I'm going to get some of the attention I want, willy or nilly." She got it, of course.

Although I saved the bedroom for the last of the packing siege, it was inevitable that Minnie's bivouac should be disturbed somewhat during the entire packing job. Luggage began to pile up in a corner. Pictures came off the walls and were temporarily stacked on the floor. And lots and lots of redundancies had to be piled into scrap baskets and taken to the incinerator. Minnie showed calm but alert interest. She did not offer to help, but she deigned to take notice of everything I did, asking "Hm-m-m?" occasionally and smiling benignly often, like a dowager pleased with her housemaid's efforts. She even picked herself up out of her corner and took up residence on a duffle bag half-filled with linens and blankets in the opposite corner. Finally, she made two attempts to cross the hall and investigate the goings-on in the hot closet, but Jo-Jo saw her coming and chased her back into the bedroom as though she had no right whatever to leave her self-imposed exile.

I was still packing in the bedroom when the movers arrived. I had borrowed my daughter's cat carrier to supplement my own, and the night before moving day, I had opened both cases and placed them on the floor in the bedroom with newspapers and clean old rags in the bottoms. Much to my surprise, as soon as Minnie had finished her breakfast on moving day, she hopped nimbly into one of the cases and relaxed. After a time, I closed the transparent cover over her, and she still made no sign of resistance.

Things were going infinitely better than I had dared to hope. She watched with interest through the cover as I stripped the bed and packed its furnishings, as the men began to take one familiar piece of furniture after another until the room was bare—and still no protest from Minnie.

SuziTu and Jo-Jo, on the other hand, began to get the jitters. By the time the apartment was empty and I had loaded my car with everything that was going in it except the cats, they were really upset. Nevertheless, they cooperated when I picked them up gently and stuffed them both into one case, where they snuggled together looking very solemn, glad of each other's close company.

Once in the car, with Minnie's case beside me on the front seat and the other one on the floor in the back, the music started, but not from my favorite suspect. Minnie lay calm and silent in her plastic-roofed house, looking out at the passing scenery. Jo-Jo and SuziTu howled for the hour and a half it took us to make the trip to our new home. There is just no predicting who is going to react how when the theory becomes actuality.

Their unpredictable behavior continued even after I had unloaded the car and introduced the cats to their new environment. Minnie, as soon as the carrying case was opened, leaped out and proceeded to explore the entire house—downstairs, upstairs, down again—uttering pleased little housewifely exclamations of "Oh, I'm going to like it here. Now isn't this a nice kitchen . . ." and such. But although SuziTu scrambled frantically from her traveling nest at the first opportunity, Jo-Jo crouched in terror on the bottom of the case until I picked him up firmly and put him on his feet. Low-slung, he scuttled out of sight, and did not reappear until the movers had left me with the mountainous job of settling in. SuziTu took up about four square inches of space behind the open front door and stayed there for several hours.

Whether Minnie, in her ancient wisdom, had planned it in advance I do not know. But the net result of her bravado from the outset and the frightened bewilderment of the other two was that Minnie had taken possession of the entire house before Jo-Jo and SuziTu had even begun to explore. "This is *mine*," said Minnie very clearly, stalking up and down the stairs on her flat feet, tossing a snarl over her shoulder when Jo-Jo timidly began to emerge for the first time and hoisting her owner's-flag tail. When she had familiarized herself with the layout of the place, found and used both boxes—the one I had placed in the downstairs powder room and the one in the upstairs bathroom—and nibbled a bite of lunch from the hastily set-up feeding station in the kitchen, she leaped nimbly up to the top of the light-garden via a chair that happened to have settled near it.

The light-garden cabinet had long been a favorite place for Jo-Jo and SuziTu because when it is lighted, there is just enough heat from the fluorescent tubes to make the plywood top comfortably warm, and they love bottom heat as much as newly planted seeds do. But since it had been in the living room of the apartment, Minnie had not had access to it during her year and a half of exile. Now she clearly intended to make up for lost time, and even though it was a couple of weeks before I got around to connecting the lights and making it warm, this was—and remains now—Minnie's private preserve. Jo-Jo and SuziTu are sometimes allowed to use it when she is not in residence, but just let one of them be there when she expects it to be unoccupied, and *someone* must go.

The first night in our new home found everyone grateful for the familiar bed with the familiar Madam in it. By this time, cautious slinking had given way to still-cautious uprightness and tentative exploration for Jo-Jo and SuziTu. Minnie kept giving them little sneers of derision at their cowardice and occasional possessive warnings about encroaching on her territory—which included the entire house. We all settled down in and on the bed as usual, and after a good night's sleep, we all awoke, eager to get started on our first day in our happy new home.

Uncertain of the procedure, but obviously anticipating the filling-in orders, all three cats waited at the head of the stairs to see what I would do first. "Breakfast, anyone?" I asked, and headed down to the kitchen. All three followed—Minnie with a confident thump-thump, which made me wonder if she remembered her stair-climbing escapades long ago in our first little apartment home together, when she had negotiated stairs in the outer hall. Jo-Jo was leery of stair-climbing in either direction, and at first took each step as a separate problem, putting first his forefeet, then his back feet, onto a tread, and repeating the slow process until he reached the first floor. SuziTu learned the technique more quickly, but still her inexperience showed in her slowness as compared with Minnie's pace.

It was a beautiful Indian-summer day, and after breakfast, I had opened both my outer doors to the fresh country air. Three eager little noses pressed against the screens; I suddenly reversed my earlier decision *not* to let them outdoors and propped the screen door open so that the cats could come and go at will. I hardly expected Minnie to venture forth, but was certain SuziTu's curiosity would lead her to investigate. To my surprise, it was Jo-Jo-the-Cautious who first left the house. And after SuziTu had taken her first tentative steps on the springy grass, even Minnie went out to sit in the sun on the top step.

Grass was another new experience, and they stepped high and slowly over it, noses down, sniffing suspiciously at it and finally nibbling it. Jo-Jo was promptly sick, but seemingly undisturbed by the experience, for he always nibbles at it when he goes out now, and almost always woopses it up again.

The first snow, however, brought out the indoor-cat preference in no uncertain terms. I opened the door to the crisp winter air and invited SuziTu to step outside. She gave me the sort of withering "are-you-*kidding?*" look that cats express so well, shook her head vigorously from side to side, and said clearly and firmly, "Na-oow!" Then she turned away from the door and raced upstairs to her favorite hot-air register, followed by a dutiful and equally nonexperimental Jo-Jo.

As the days went on and our house gradually became a home, the cats unfolded like little blossoms. They learned to race up and down the stairs without fear of a misstep, although I can always tell who is coming. Minnie's flat forefeet make a distinctive thump. Jo-Jo has a firm but hippity-hop tread. And light-footed SuziTu skitters.

The integration that Minnie had advertently or inadvertently established at the outset continues with variations. No longer an isolationist at all, she obviously believes she has first rights wherever she may choose to be, as it was before the Revolt. In the beginning of our new life, she would not allow the other two to join her at the feeding station, snarling them away or angrily taking her departure if they insisted on their own rights. But after a few days, when I gave them a meal they really love, she forgot her prejudices, and now they all line up under the kitchen table without regard for protocol—or each other.

Madam's attention, though, is another matter. The minute

I sit down, there is a race between Minnie and Jo-Jo, wherever they may happen to be, to see who can get onto my lap first. Sometimes Minnie makes it and turns to sneer aloud at Jo-Jo, who cuddles close beside me and silently swears at her with hating eyes. Sometimes he wins the race, and Minnie crouches close beside me, trying to look pathetic and unloved until I pet her. When this happens, Jo-Jo often reaches out with a tentative brown paw toward her upturned face. I am never quite certain whether he intends to pat her affectionately or to give her a fast swat. So I take his paw in my hand and prevent any further aggression by petting them both, showing no favoritism.

SuziTu continues her laissez-faire policy and, whenever possible, avoids any controversial situations. One night she was trapped. She had taken advantage of Minnie's apparent content on my lap and seized the rare opportunity to warm herself on the top of the light-garden. When I got up from my seat, telling Minnie I would not be back for a while, Minnie made a beeline for the light-garden, where she arrived with a startled snarl when she found SuziTu there ahead of her. Since SuziTu could not leave her perch without passing close to Minnie, she curled her feet under her as tightly as possible, turned apologetic blue eyes toward Minnie, and remained where she was. Minnie, recovering from the initial shock of invaded privacy, settled down quietly with her back to SuziTu. There is really plenty of room there, even with two big pots of Amaryllis taking up some of the space. Later, SuziTu had made her escape without loss of dignity, I guess, because I found Minnie alone and had heard no commotion. SuziTu is a pacifist, and sometimes even a peacemaker.

Jo-Jo clearly is of two minds about how to treat Minnie. He has not forgotten that she snubbed him first, and occasionally he sets out quite deliberately to annoy her. Sometimes I hear the two of them coming down the stairs at a rapid clip, and I know exactly what is going on: Jo-Jo is steering an interference course. He runs along beside Minnie, very close, peering into her face and echoing every turn she makes, like a football player trying to divert the guy with the ball who is headed toward the goal line. Minnie tries with great dignity to ignore him and hastens her pace; but this is a game Jo-Jo loves "because he knows it teases."

Sometimes, too, when Minnie is peacefully sitting on the sofa minding her own business, Jo-Jo approaches with slinking step and wickedly gleaming eye. Standing close, directly before her, he reaches up with his forepaw in slow motion, shoving his face into hers. Her immediate reaction is to flatten her ears, roll onto her right shoulder (most cats are southpaws), and raise her left paw in fighting position. From there, anything can happen, but nothing ever does. There is a low mutter of swearing from both of them; maybe Jo-Jo's fur rises along his spine and tail, and maybe Minnie beats a hasty retreat. They do not come to blows, but Jo-Jo has had his fun at routing his victim. Of course I reprimand him, and he gives me an innocently wide-eyed "who-me?" stare, but at least he knows that I know what he is up to, and it has a somewhat restraining influence.

Our new home is complete with an extensive lawn, a duck pond, and right next door, a horse corral with two horses who do not always care to stay inside their fence. There are also six children, a big Collie named Chris of Christmas Corners, and at least three cats. Accordingly, I confined my cats' first ventures into the great outdoors to the back entrance, which opens out toward the duck pond and the woods, rather than toward Chris's domain. The five enormous white ducks who are special pets of my neighbors have eleven wild mallard friends, and thirteen wild wood ducks who visit frequently. They are all very tame and friendly birds who set up a noisy clamor every time they hear my door open. "Got anything for us?" they ask, coming eagerly out of the water.

I thought it would do no harm to introduce the cats to them, but the ducks are so large that the poor cats were terrified, and my fears that the birds might have problems with my felines were unfounded. The cats give them a very wide berth.

Chris, accustomed to his own cat family, has no evil intent toward mine. But instinct is strong, and the first time SuziTu ventured into his territory, picking her way with cautious jauntiness up the driveway toward Christmas Corners, Chris lifted his shaggy head to stare at her, but said nothing. SuziTu, catching sight of him, turned around and fairly flew home. She barely missed colliding with the outward-opened screen door, scuttled around it and through the doorway, never stopping until she had traversed the entire length of the living room and found safety under the sofa. The next day I offered her the opportunity to venture forth again through the same front door, but she tossed a frightened look in the direction of Chris's house and once again scurried under the living room sofa. She is braver now, but it took a bit of Chris-ignores-her time.

One day while I was outdoors doing yard work, SuziTu came out to tell me how much she enjoys country living. She frisked about me for a time, and then, like any little girl full of play, carefully balanced herself on the narrow foundation ledge and picked her way along it like a fence-walker, shouting "Wa-oow! Wa-oow!" She circled the house three times, shouting gleefully, as though it were a symbolic rite.

Jo-Jo is quieter in his enjoyment of the outdoor life. Sometimes I see him slowly picking his way across the lawn toward the tiny river that edges it. When he has finished his explorations, if he returns to a closed door, he scratches gently until I open up and let him in, or utters a soft "Aa-ow" to announce himself. He is braver out of doors than I had expected him to be. I *should not* be surprised, perhaps, because his major fear is claustrophobia and there is much open space outdoors.

Even Minnie likes to walk around in the grass a bit, usually to a nice sunny spot where she can sit quietly inspecting the view around her.

One night when I had a friend to dinner, we heard Jo-Jo complaining bitterly that he was lost. (Every cat has his own individual worry-sound, and anyone who lives with him learns to recognize it.) Investigating, I found him in plain view in the middle of the staircase. "Jo-Jo," I said, "you're not lost. What's wrong?"

"Lost!" he repeated, and looked worriedly at me.

"Where's SuziTu?" I asked in sudden inspiration. "Is she lost?"

Jo-Jo started up the stairs. My friend and I followed, and the three of us searched the entire house, looking under the furniture, opening all the closets, calling, "SuziTu, where are you?"

No answer from SuziTu, and finally I widened the search to the gathering dusk outside. Still she did not answer my call, and even when I called her a half hour later, convinced that she was outdoors in the blackness that had fallen by then, I got no response. I had horrible visions of what might happen to her and was not particularly relieved when I saw the big white angora cat from Christmas Corners beating a hasty retreat toward home.

Another half hour passed before I heard SuziTu's voice at the front door. Jo-Jo was there before me, and as I opened the door, he chased her up the stairs to the bedroom, where they spent the rest of the evening in silence. I do not know whether she confessed all about her great adventure, but certainly I will never know where she was.

I try not to let the cats out at night. For their inexperience, we are near too many dangers—ranging from wild foxes who sometimes invade the henhouses nearby to wild drivers who tear up and down the bordering roads.

Now my cat family has new favorite places. Often when I am sitting in the living room with Minnie by my side, we hear a wild scramble about us, and I say, "That's the people upstairs." Minnie smiles at me, knowing that the people upstairs are chasing each other in a game of tag inspired by sheer exuberance. It is only when we are all in bed and still hear the sound of scurrying feet above us that the cats and I look up, wondering who the people upstairs really are. Accustomed to apartment living, we still recognize the difference between familiar footsteps and those of squirrels or field mice who may be wintering in the crawl-space above our second floor. The cats show wild excitement at these sounds, but there is no way for them to get at the under-the-roof intruders, whoever they may be.

One favorite place is my dressing room, because the two hot-air registers keep it almost too cozy, no matter how firmly I try to turn them off and keep the heat downstairs where I want it. Often I find SuziTu and Jo-Jo both sitting over the registers in the dressing-room floor, and as often, SuziTu reminds me (by nesting there) that it is on the shelf in the back corner, where I store fabric remnants and other soft things, that she intends to have her next nursery. It is such an ideal place for kittens that I shall go along with her request, when I find a suitable father for her kittens—on a borrowing basis.

For Minnie, the favorite place second only to her light-garden perch is wherever I am working. Usually it is at my desk in the Brown Study, but occasionally I spread papers out on the kitchen table. Wherever there are papers, there Minnie wants to sit. It ends in rather a profusion of fairly orderly piles of finished and unfinished work, since nothing will budge the big black body that has planted itself sprawlingly before me. She will stay there for hours at a time, until I leave my desk, when she jumps down immediately to follow at my heels to my next lighting place.

Jo-Jo is still the restless one, pacing the floor and seldom staying very long in one place unless he can be close to SuziTu. But he is fascinated by our first-floor windows, from which he can watch the ducks parade in single file toward the big house where they are fed night and morning. And from one window he can see the horses looking longingly over the fence toward our apple trees. Now that we are settled, his mirror game continues, too, with the mirrors in different but accessible places that still fascinate him.

Altogether, I can say with confidence that my city cats have become country cats with no regrets whatever.

13

As Cats Go Marching On

A year has passed since Minnie's kidney trouble sent her to the hospital for the last time. Now I can talk about her again. Yet from time to time, I still imagine I hear her flat-footed thuds on the stair treads, and sometimes when I wake in the night, feeling a warm little body curved against mine, I think it is hers. No matter how many times we suffer the loss of a dear friend, each is a separate little tragedy by itself.

It is comforting to know that most of Minnie's life was brimming with happiness and comfort. Especially in her last months, when she had come back into her own as matriarch of the cat family, and within the limitations of her old age, she was able to enjoy the new experiences of country life. She was happy then, as she had been in her life with Monster. She had lived out her time, and I think she went to her final sleep with a soft purr in her contented heart.

While I was waiting in the hospital for the doctor to complete his examination, I asked his nurse if she knew of a possible mate for SuziTu. SuziTu was again most urgently wanting to be a mother, and I could find no reason for objecting. As it happened, the nurse did know a handsome Siamese tom named Pharaoh, who was scheduled to be neutered very shortly. If I wanted his services before it was too late, I should get on the phone and make a date with his people.

I did so, and Pharaoh's people said they would be happy to have SuziTu immediately as a house guest. In order to minimize the trauma of their being separated from each other, I loaded Jo-Jo into the carrying case with his little mate and took him along—not to stay for her visit with Pharaoh, but to understand that she was not going on a one-way trip to the hospital, as he knew Minnie had.

Pharaoh was as he had been described, and a bit more. He took off after SuziTu as though he had been shot from a cannon, and she retreated under unfamiliar furniture, snarling at him. Jo-Jo watched through the plastic roof of the carrying case in complete silence. Eventually, we went home, Jo-Jo and I, leaving SuziTu to her fate, with a final injunction "Think kittens, Suzi, think kittens."

A week later, I went alone to bring our hopefully expectant mother home. Pharaoh's people reported that he had rudely lost interest in her a couple of days ago, and either she was pregnant or she never would be, as far as Pharaoh was concerned. He was to lose his masculinity the following week.

When SuziTu jumped out of the carrying case in her own home, Jo-Jo was beside himself with joy. You would have thought he had done the deed himself, from the way he galloped back and forth around the house, raced up and down the stairs, shouting gleefully, with tail hoisted in triumph. SuziTu was equally pleased to see him and said so with fond little caresses and soft sounds. She had not been an ideal house guest, I gathered from Pharaoh's people, although they were very kind about it. She had not only had a rousing battle with Pharaoh's own already pregnant mate, but she had apparently misbehaved and sulked throughout her entire visit, rousing herself to normal affection and sweet disposition only when she saw me again. So now there was nothing to do but mark my calendar with the date of expected birth, if any, and hope for the best. Continuously, I told her to "think kittens"–having parodied the phrase from my daughter's "think snow" during the skiing season–and she smiled and purred happily, looking concentratedly thoughtful each time I said it.

It was not long before I knew with certainty that she was going to have kittens sometime between April 20th and April 26th. She was as happy about it as she had been about the other two litters, and Jo-Jo was affectionate, attentive, and proud. She began to bulge. She grew–and grew–and grew. Never before had she been so vastly expanded in pregnancy, and I was delighted. "Either she's going to have a tremendous litter," I predicted, "or she'll have really big kittens." I did not know how right I was, or even guess that it might create a problem. Because my garden was beginning to burgeon with spring flowers, I decided on names for a litter of six: Crocus, Daffodil, Tulip, Hyacinth, Snowdrop, and Forsythia.

As her time drew near, I arranged my schedule so that I would be home to help her whenever possible, knowing she would expect it, and each morning that I had to leave to go to work in the city, I cautioned her to wait until my return. She smiled reassuringly. But the days went on, and I grew anxious. Had she never before been a mother, it would be no matter for exceptional concern if she were a few days late. But this was the third time, and I began to worry a bit. So it was enormously comforting to learn that Pharaoh's regular mate had had her litter a week late, too.

Since SuziTu's previous babies had been born in the city apartment, she and I had debated at length about where her nursery should be this time. We agreed that there was much to be said for my dressing room. It is warm, dark, secluded, and near my bed. But on the other hand, it is upstairs, and perhaps it would be easier for SuziTu to keep the kittens on the first floor until they were old enough to climb stairs. So we weighed the possibilities of a corner in the furnace room. She considered the location so favorable that I slept for two nights on the couch in the adjacent Brown Study, thinking she might have the babies there and then. The third night, however, she led me purposefully upstairs to my own bed and lured me into the dressing room to point out her ultimate, firm choice.

In case she should change her mind at the last minute or get caught short, I left her familiar upholstered carton next to the furnace and set up a luxurious new birthing bed where we could both reach it on a shelf in the dressing room. She approved, but still the babies did not come. I settled down to wait a few more days, and it was the evening of May third when SuziTu climbed into her nest, purring loudly, her contractions very evident.

I hovered, putting unnecessary final touches on her surroundings, waiting. And waiting. These kittens were taking longer than usual, and I dared not leave her for a moment. She continued to purr happily, but soon I realized that the sac had broken, which meant a dry birth and possible trouble. I phoned for the vet. His answering service promised to locate him and have him call back. I returned to SuziTu and changed her bedding. She was still smiling and purring happily, but I knew she was in trouble. I talked to her reassuringly, not wanting to communicate my increasing fears.

It was close to midnight when the answering service reported complete failure in locating the doctor. I knew I was going to have to be SuziTu's only medic, and I felt terribly inadequate. As I hung up the phone, SuziTu flopped out of her bed and began dragging herself across the floor, a grotesque half-born kitten hampering her progress. Without thought, I grabbed the cold, limp body of the kitten, and held on while SuziTu struggled away from it. She turned a frightened snarl onto her stillborn infant and leapt onto my bed. I plucked her off and carried her back to her own nest, where she promptly gave birth to a beautifully normal, very much alive kitten. I congratulated her, admired her baby, and made sure she was not bleeding before I went back to examine the cause of her ordeal. I was nearly hysterical, but I had to keep SuziTu from worry and could only hope that she was physically as undamaged as she appeared to be psychologically.

The problem kitten had been, I remembered, a breach birth; but it was also a monster. About twice the size of a normal kitten, and possibly misshapen as well, it was just more than SuziTu's little slender body could bear. Almost sick with relief that she herself was apparently all right, I finally went wearily to bed. Her labor had lasted six hours.

Twice during that night she waked me and coaxed me into the dressing room. Each time, I thought perhaps by some miracle she had borne another kitten, but all she wanted was to show me her one little prize. She was as proud of her solitary baby as though it were the six I had expected and hoped for. I named it Crocus-Daffodil-Hyacinth-Tulip-Snowdrop-Forsythia, and gave it the nickname of "Mac" right from the outset.

When I took Mac to get her shots, I asked Dr. Dann what could have gone wrong with SuziTu and Pharaoh's litter. By that time I had learned from Pharaoh's people that, even to their own surprise, Pharaoh weighed eleven pounds, and I thought it possible that his bones and hard muscle, so much heftier than SuziTu's, might have had something to do with it. Dr. Dann said there were numerous things that could have gone wrong, and there was actually no way of knowing just what had caused this misconception. "It's always a risk," he said, "to mate any animals. But on the other hand, it might never have happened. There's no reason whatever to think that SuziTu would necessarily or even probably have the same thing happen again. But if you want her altered, of course we'll do it when Mac has been weaned." I have not done it yet.

Mac was a big girl when she was born, a week late, and she grew and developed very rapidly. Her eyes opened on the third day; she was climbing out of her nest long before any of her predecessors had ventured forth; and she was from birth a charmer. Never having known city life, it was natural for her to want to be outdoors whenever possible. She learned at an early age to negotiate the stairs to the first floor, and it was only a matter of days after that before she taught herself to go in and out of the house through the swinging panel designed for the cats and built low into a screen door.

On one of her first outdoor excursions, Mac met Chris, our Collie neighbor, under rather difficult circumstances. Chris had been snoozing in a favorite place under the little evergreen tree that grows beside my front porch. Jo-Jo, SuziTu, and Mac came strolling through the opened screen door from the porch just as Chris, yawning widely and stretching his big body, arose from his hiding place. Not seeing him yet, Jo-Jo took off for the grape arbor, while Mac began an exploratory jaunt around the corner of the house. Her mother paused in the doorway, and Chris took her unaware by appearing unexpectedly not a foot away.

SuziTu's mother instinct prompted a warning yowl to Mac, who immediately tried to climb the side of the house. Jo-Jo came scurrying out of the grape arbor just as Chris and SuziTu converged on little Mac, whose climb had ended in predictable disaster. Mac was on her back on the ground. Chris leaned his long Collie nose over her to see what in the world had fallen off the house so suddenly, and Mac produced her tiny sharp claws. Chris, whose best friends are cats, was in serious danger with all three ganged up on him, and there was a brief moment of bedlam as I, tugging at his coat and screaming, "Chris! Chris! No, Chris . . ." tried to fend off the two adult cats and scoop up the kitten. So Mac has been growing up with no fear of dogs—or anything else, for that matter.

She races up and down trees. She catches birds, I am sorry to say. She early learned to imitate her mother's stunt of jumping onto my back. She does everything any Siamese cat ever thought of doing, and a few things that I am sure originated with her. But she does them better, faster, more vigorously than any cat who has ever lived with me. When she chases her mother, who is no slouch in a race, Mac gets so close to SuziTu's retreating rear that she jumps over her parent and turns around to see if the intended prey is following.

But all has not been complete harmony in our family since Mac was born. During SuziTu's pregnancy, Jo-Jo was the ever-doting mate. During that long and difficult birth process, Jo-Jo worried as he had worried about the previous litters—his own progeny. But the moment of truth came to him with his first sniff at Mac. There was an expression close to repugnance as he turned to me and said with a cold glance, "I had nothing to do with this kitten." He turned from SuziTu's nest and stalked away.

Aside from pretending that there was no kitten, for as long as it was possible to ignore that very difficult-to-ignore baby, he was markedly and increasingly cool to SuziTu. Until he reached the point of snarling openly, she did nothing more than look hurt and preoccupied; but when he began to snarl each time he saw her, SuziTu put him in his place with a sharp-clawed swat across his nose. The unfriendliness ripened into frequent battles, with Madam trying to mediate, to pacify, to cajole. They would not be mediated. They would not be pacified. They would not be cajoled. They would be enemies until Jo-Jo gave in and took Mac unto his bosom. Which, he swore angrily, he would never, never do.

Unwittingly, I found the answer not only to this particular feud, but also to the one that inevitably developed between Mac and her mother when Mac was weaned. I went away for a long weekend, leaving the cats alone in care of my favorite cat-sitter from next door. When I returned, the blobs of fur that littered the staircase were mute evidence of what had been going on in my absence. But Jo-Jo and SuziTu were curled up together in fond embrace on the sofa. And Jo-Jo was taking friendly note of Mac as well. Without Madam to turn to for sympathy—or to interfere, with well-meant efforts at reconciliation—they had solved their problem by themselves.

All of SuziTu's kittens heretofore had gone to other homes as soon as their mother became restless with them.

Mac just continued to stick around as though she intended to stay forever, which was my plan for her from the outset. This program did not in the least fit in, however, with SuziTu's intentions of at last being queen bee in her family, and she set about correcting the situation. She was determined, it appeared, to make her daughter leave home if Madam was not going to get rid of her.

As maliciously as she had harangued Jo-Jo once he had aroused her ire, she snarled and spat and swatted at the innocent little Mac, who, such a short time before, had been her baby—happily nursing, snuggling, and playing. Mac said nothing, but kept a watchful eye on her mother's paws. When Mac wanted love, she came to me. She was never pathetic about it, and I admired her spirit of independence, seeming at so young an age to recognize that she had a perfect right to make her home with us. And if SuziTu wanted to be unpleasant about it, SuziTu could jolly well go climb a tree.

But once again, alone-togetherness ironed out their differences. Another long weekend was apparently fraught with battle activities, but Mac had worked out a most effective buttering-up technique. SuziTu was in heat again, howling loudly and rolling in her sexiest manner. Whenever she settled down for a moment, Mac, now almost as large as SuziTu, snuggled in kittenish fashion against her mother and actually pretended to nurse. This attention pleased SuziTu so enormously that she retrogressed at once into her motherly attitude and forgave her daughter without reservations for continuing to live with us.

I found this suckling program a trifle disgusting, probably because Mac was being a complete phony, and so was SuziTu, who of course had no milk to offer her great big "little one." But I decided I had interfered enough, and if my techniques for achieving harmony did not work, and theirs did, I should think twice before I made suggestions. So everybody is happy again, at least most of the time. Jo-Jo gives unstinting affection and attention to his adored SuziTu, but he also shows a certain warmth toward Mac, surpassing mere tolerance but falling short of his devotion to her mother, which of course is proper. Mac has a little gleam of "I-know-you-two" in her eyes whenever she looks at her elders, but aside from always doing exactly what she feels like when she feels like doing it, heedless of anyone's advice, she never initiates an argument. She plays with the older cats when she sees they are not going to object and leaves them to their own devices when she knows they might take offense at her teasing.

This is as happy a family group as could be planned, and last week when SuziTu had her fifth birthday, I decided that very soon I will give her a present of dubious joy. I am going to have her spayed so that she and Jo-Jo can enjoy each other's company without the strain that becomes obvious when she is in heat and he tries so gallantly and unsuccessfully to please her. SuziTu has been a wonderful mother of wonderful kittens, but Jo-Jo was a happy father only when he really was their father. And there is still no conclusive knowledge in veterinary science about the continuing health of an unmated, unspayed female. Some scientists believe this condition leads to uterine cysts and tumors, so why take a chance?

Mac, maturing slowly as is normal with her breed, has not yet showed interest in motherhood. But she does grow more and more feminine in her walk, in her little flirtatious tail-wavings, and in an increasing desire to roll over and look alluring. She is growing up, and when she does, I would like her to mate with a full Siamese, for she is sturdy and physically far superior to her mother. When she is ready to have kittens, Mac will have a bunch of little jet streamliners and be a mother in SuziTu's tradition, if I choose her mate with discretion. Since she is Pharaoh's daughter, and I shall want to keep one of her sons, I have already chosen his name. It could not be anything other than Moses. And how will SuziTu react to being Moses's grandma?

Aside from the cats in my own family, things have also happened among my cat friends. Othello, for example, reverted to his nomadic tendencies and left my Central New York friends to go and take up residence on a neighboring farm. He gives us a friendly greeting when we see him there, but makes no offer to come back. Once a nomad, perhaps always a nomad. . . .

And next door at Christmas Corners, the three cats who were so beloved by the six children have all met death in different ways. One died of eating a shrew, which has a unique poison fatal to cats. One died of an infected paw, which refused to respond to the latest medical treatments. And the beautiful albino angora, most beloved of all because she was stone deaf, had extra toes on all her feet, and sported one blue eye and one green, succumbed to her second paralytic stroke when she was nine years old.

But nature has a way of compensating for such losses, especially when a family is headed, like this one, by understanding, cat-and-child-loving parents. A little tabby kitten, purchased at a church fair (which is still another place to look when you want another pet) entered the family about the time that SuziTu had her shortchanged litter. I had promised one of her kittens to the children, and of course even their frequent visits to Mac did not make up for their need for a kitten of their own. And two days after the elderly white cat's last stroke, the little tabby had to be rushed to the hospital during a heavy snowstorm to have her three kittens (one stillborn) by Cesarean section.

"I never thought I'd be taking a cat for prenatal care," remarked the father of the six children; but he was as eager as any of us for those kittens to be born, and the prenatal examination confirmed that the little mother would not be able to have her kittens normally. Her pelvis had been crushed when she was run over by a car before she was more than half grown. She must have heard us planning her alteration, for she disappeared to spend the night on the town about the time she was to be spayed. One of the kittens is a red-striped tom, and the other, a glossy black female. Four-year-old Bobbie named them Handsome and Gretel.

We who love animals as individuals never forget them as individuals. Each has a special place in our hearts. And when that place becomes a memory box, the newer additions to our sphere of affection are precisely that–additions, not replacements. To a cat lover, there will always be cats–past, present, and future–twenty-four hours a day.